I Can Eat Boogers Too

Other books by this author:

LEAVING NEVERLAND (WHY LITTLE BOYS SHOULDN'T RUN BIG CORPORATIONS)

Reviews:
"An insightful depiction of the dangers we face in having the perpetual 'boys' of this world in positions of power – incomplete men with arrested development. The style, pace and delightful skewering are reminiscent of Hunter S Thomson!" Rex Finch, Finch Publishing.

"You really cracked me up - I couldn't stop laughing. My husband honestly thought I'd lost the plot... such an entertaining read." K. K. Jones author of 'Hens from Hell'

"I wanted to tell you that this is a very clever piece of writing, highlighting important issues in a unique way through using Peter Pan, and the Neverland scenario." Marita Hansen, author of 'Behind the Hood'

Genre: Non-fiction. Rites of Passage, Growing Up
ISBN: 978-0-9808288-0-1 252 pages

TAKING IT WITH YOU

Everybody knows you can't take anything with you when you die… almost everybody.

To heir is human, to try to be your own heir? Madness. In a fit of rage a dying, spiritually challenged woman vows to take her vast fortune with her when she dies. Somehow. Unfortunately, cryonics leaves her cold but when she stumbles on the fact that the Tibetan Buddhists have found the Dalai Lama's reincarnation 13 times, she becomes obsessed with leaving everything to herself. She reasons that for a very large sum of money, surely, the Tibetans would find her reincarnation once.

Reviews: "Intoxicatingly delicious, inspirational read. I found this book hard to put down. I thoroughly enjoyed it." Panda, Goodreads Review

"You will laugh, cry, cringe, feel humbled and inspired. This is a simple but great story that looks at some of life's big questions in a humorous and inspiring way. I would recommend this book to anyone." Inspired Reader, Amazon Review

Genre: Fiction ISBN: 978-0-9808288-4-9 252 pages

I Can Eat Boogers Too

Parenting stories to warm the cockles of your heart… and wet the tip of your finger

By

Daniel Prokop

Published by
Continuum Australia Pty Ltd

www.danielprokop.com
daniel@leavingneverland.net

www.facebook.com/I Can Eat Boogers Too

Copyright © Daniel Prokop 2015
Cover design by Aesthetica Society

National Library of Australia
Cataloguing- in- Publication data

Creator: Prokop, Daniel, author
Title: I Can Eat Boogers Too: Parenting Stories to Warm the Cockles of your Heart .. and wet the tip of your finger / Daniel Prokop.

ISBN: 978 0 9808288-6-3

Subjects: Parenthood—Humor, Parenting –Humor,
Parent and child --Humor
Dewey Number: 649.1

BISAC Codes:FAM034000 Family & Relationships/Parenting/General
FAM020000 Family & Relationships/Parenting/ Fatherhood
HUM011000 Humor/Topic/Marriage & Families

All rights reserved. Apart from any fair dealing for the purposes of private study, research, criticism or review, as permitted under the Copyright Act, no part may be reproduced or stored by any process or means without written permission. Inquiries should be made to the author.

For Sam and Aelysha, thank you for being in my life. I am a very lucky Dad. I love you both to the stars and back a googol times.

Table of Contents

Forward   by Robin Grille

1. I Can Eat Boogers Too   11
2. Then He was Five   15
3. The Naming   21
4. Black Five   25
5. Legal Eaglets   31
6. I said Housework not Hogwarts   37
7. When Kissing It Better Stops   41
8. The Boy Who Punched the Sky   43
9. I Love You Like a Rock   47
10. The Cuddle Bank   53
11. The Power of Please   59
12. Thinking of Thank You   64
13. Samuel's Sand   70
14. The Pillock   72
15. Wedgey Snake   80
16. In a Sandpit Not so Far Away   86
17. Wrestling Dad for the Win   90
18. T'was Christmas Day + other treats   94
19. Parent Teacher Teacher Child   101
20 Where has my Pedestal Gone?   109
21. The Parent Olympics   119
22. Dancing with Whales   124
23 First Steps: If You Can't Walk Properly…   128
24. Great Parental Expectations   136
25. Father's Day Note to my First Born   140
Parenting Books I Love   142

Forward by Robin Grille

My Dad was my hero when I was a little boy. I told everyone I was going to be an engineer just like my Dad. And though today I am most un-engineer-like, I remember that feeling like it was yesterday.

Hallowed ground, this place called Fatherhood; privileged position, terrifying responsibility; a temporary hero to small humans that we love beyond reason. We hold them in our awe. And for a few short years, they think we are the bees' knees.

In our children's company, we play like we haven't played since we were kids. We laugh louder. We act silly. We stuff up, monumentally. We are sorry. We embarrass ourselves. We exaggerate our prowess: We lie a little. We make up the rules. We wrestle. We get hit in the balls – a lot (which I believe is evolutionary: this is how kids try to eliminate the competition: The most primitive form of sibling rivalry. Think about it). We are brave, and we are foolhardy. As Dads, we do our own stunts. And despite the scars, bruises and ego-dents…we are better persons for it. That is our children's mission. They help us to grow; simply by being themselves, and by being there (aka in our face).

Do the other Dads - the ones from your board-room, your workshop, your office – know the real you? Do they know who you become when you get home and dive into kid world? Do they know your tenderness, your huge heart, your clumsiness, your absurdity, your inner clown? And how well do you know your male friends as fathers?

I think that is what Daniel Prokop's little book (this one, you're holding it) is all about. He shows you himself as a Dad, you are a fly on his wall. And you see yourself in these pages, sooner or later. It's a warm, laughter-filled, no-holds-barred journey through the everyday glories and agonies of parenting: From the grand to the ridiculous, from the heart-rending to the maddening, naked and true. Look in this mirror and you see a bit of all of us. And you feel a bit less alone, like it is all even more worthwhile. It's about more than parenting, it is about membership of a big, beautiful, world-wide club.

You can read this in your special chair. You can read this in the shed. You can even read it on the loo. Daniel talks straight and believes in fun. He does not want to patronize you with answers, just to invite you into a shared experience. From swimming with whales, to imparting the etiquette of mucous, from setting boundaries to hugging the kids tight, I think you will enjoy these cheeky vignettes. Don't be surprised if your inner child reads too, over your shoulder.

Robin Grille is the internationally acclaimed author of *'Parenting for a Peaceful World'* **and** *'Heart to Heart Parenting'*. **He is an inspiring speaker, a passionate social change activist and he takes a very strong stand for those that can only sit or crawl.**

Robin has been in private practice as a psychologist for over twenty years' and he is a dedicated parent educator. Robin's extensive research has led him to feel that improved attention to babies' and children's emotional needs is the most powerful way to move societies toward sustainability and peace.

1

I Can Eat Boogers Too

Booger: dried nasal mucus
Mucus: pronunciation: mū′kŭs
Noun. **1**. *(Physiol.)* A viscid fluid secreted by mucous membranes, which it serves to moisten and protect. It covers the lining membranes of all the cavities which open externally **2**. *(Snack)* Often found being consumed discreetly at traffic lights and with great vigor in school playgrounds.

I told my 4 year old daughter that little girls don't put their fingers in their nostrils, that only horrible, yucky boys pick their noses and then eat their boogers. For a little while, I think she actually believed me. Certainly she didn't park a digit there the way some young lads do and luck was with me as she didn't see the filthy look that my wife shot me for telling such a porky pie.

After a sticky afternoon spent researching snot on the web I found that surprisingly few studies have been performed on nose picking, but that up to 91% of adults in one survey admitted that they picked their nose. To me it was a surprising result; I thought that more than 9 % of adults were liars.

I tell my kids that they are lucky; that at their age they can do deep, deep drilling; second knuckle mining and get away with it.

"Enjoy the freedom," I say, "Because as an adult you will be restricted to a quick pick and a flick if you are lucky." I go on to explain: "Kids, the shortening of the depth and duration of nose picking is not just due to emotional choking. It is also part physiology because bigger fingers deny an adult the unrestricted access to the remote extremities of the nasal cavity that you guys obviously enjoy exploring."

"Keep listening to me children because this is important. Breathing is fundamental to life. Three minutes without air and you will black out and can suffer minor brain damage, after four to five minutes you can die. Breathing is vital, much more essential than drinking water or eating food so culturally you would think that scraping dried mucous out of an air passage with a finger nail would be encouraged."

"Sadly kids, in most families, public picking is not sanctioned but in our family we have no such taboos. You can go out and play now, you little scamps, but just remember that regular maintenance and cleaning of your nasal passages is even more important than having fun."

My little heart to heart talks generally reduce finger to nose contact quite considerably. Encouraging them to really go for it somehow takes the pleasure out of it for them. Isn't it wonderful when reverse psychology actually works?

At night when I am putting my son to sleep I can nearly always get a giggle out of him if I look up his nose and ask him if he's saving a couple of those big juicy nose nuggets for a mid-night snack.

"Ohhh, Dad!" A quick punch to my arm and then he dives under the bedclothes where he does a quick audit to check whether I am teasing or not.

It is fair to say that I was pretty smug on the topic of snot until one day, yes, I got slimed, smacked myself right in my self-satisfied facial protuberance. Me, the Bogeyman of Boogers, the Policeman of Pickers got sprung badly.

How do I explain it? Well, I was trying to get out of the house when I realized that I had a hanger, a cornflake right up there that was making my left nostril itch. I was already late for a meeting. I checked my pockets for tissues or a handkerchief. No socially approved nasal cleaning peripherals were found. Dammit.

It was an important meeting and I was in a big hurry and so I committed myself to a quick maintenance pick. For my trouble I ended up with a small trophy but nowhere to mount it. Call me crazy, but somehow I didn't feel like flicking it on the floor or wiping it on my suit.

I didn't think anyone was around, so I did what anyone would do in my situation; I gobbled that sucker down and got ready to race out the door quietly confident that no one in the meeting would ever suspect me of munching my own mucous.

That was when I heard: "Dad? Did you just eat a booger?"

I felt like a trapped rat. I crouched down trying to make myself smaller. I may have even squeaked. I immediately reached for a lie, any lie to get me out of this terrible situation. I primed a number of almost truths; "I don't know what you are talking about," "I missed it;" and the classic "I was only scratching."

This was potentially a multi-lie situation. Multi-lie scenarios are ones where one primary lie is backed up with a number of secondary lies. A deep guilt infection pushes the first lie out before the brain can engage and even though the liar knows that sticking with the primary lie, no matter how bad it is, is always the best policy, a deep guilt infection will nearly always push up the rancid puss of secondary lies.

Credibility is inversely proportional to the number of secondary lies. A gold medal secondary lie will never make up for a poor primary lie. I wouldn't know myself, of course, but this is what I have observed or rather what a friend told me, no wait, I mean this is what my Grandpa, no my Grandma told me or one of my siblings, I think, or maybe I read it on the internet or now I remember, I got it sent as spam. See?

So there I was, busted, with the proverbial smoking gun of my still moist finger still poised in the air. I did the impossible, I dug deep and I looked my son straight in the eyes and I said with a grin, "It was delicious." Sam started giggling and I started giggling, I gave him a hug and headed out the door for my meeting.

If we can't be straight with our young people about nose picking then what hope have we got when they start asking the hard questions about sex, and drugs?

Author's note: I have been asked by myself to note an article for readers from the Huffington Post: *Never Mind 'Don't Pick Your Nose' -- Boogers May Be Good for You* **by Dr. Joseph Mercola.**

2

Then He Was Five

My wife Beth and I celebrated 5 years of being parents with a party. We got the official thumbs up from our son Sam which was important because the party was to celebrate his birthday. One of the excited children said as he was leaving, "I wish we could all come to your birthday party every day, Sam!" Yeah, right.

We did have quite a few magic moments on the day. When Sam woke up we said, "Happy Birthday our five year old!"

Sam looked down at his body and in wonder said, "Am I five now?"

We said, "Yes!"

"But I'm not any bigger?"

I'm not quite sure if he expected to wake up with a goatee and mustache but I guess he'd kind of figured that at that magic age of five - bingo - you're all grown up.

As party time approached Beth and I both felt the pressure to perform. We had worked hard but we were virgins when it came to event managing a child's birthday party. We knew that the jury would be sympathetic but we also knew that our jurors were a gaggle of pre-school veterans. A social gaffe now and we could add another zero to Sam's future therapy bills.

We had done our research; we knew that salted snacks and sugar would be our friends on this day. Our mission: use the substances in such a cunning way that we retain the social goodwill from the dispensing of the confectionery whilst ensuring that the big sugar hit and the associated behavioral challenges kick in only after the children have left our premises. This meant, of course, that our timing had to be spot on.

At the pre-party planning session we synchronised watches, read through the children's resumes and went through the agenda… one last time. A final mad dash to put up balloons and streamers and it was show time - the video was rolling.

We stretched the time we had allocated to meet, greet and commence general room trashing to 15 minutes. Salted snacks were dispensed, sugar kept carefully in reserve.

We had conferred with a number of party consultants (other parents) who had all agreed that allocating 20-25 minutes for the cardboard dodgem car races was conservative. The 'cars' were cardboard boxes that we had painted and cut holes in the bottom of so the boys could step into the cars and hold the 'chassis' up by adjusting the custom fitted cloth shoulder straps that doubled as seatbelts: Safety first, safety last.

We lined the drivers up and I blew the whistle, "Cars on!" In the ensuing excited jostling for pole position disaster struck with yowls and whimpers. The safety warden had missed the pre-race shoe check and our yard was full of tiny, evil prickly burrs (bindies). We had no choice but to send up a shoe recovery mission.

By the time all the malignant bindies had been extracted and all of the shoes and sandals had found feet it was obvious that we had lost momentum. No amount of whistle blowing, creative cajoling or race officials running thoughtfully through the track marked by bright orange cardboard witches hats could keep the dodgems going for more than 5 minutes.

This was a major setback. Our wealth of inexperience had not prepared us for this contingency. In the hurried crisis meeting that followed we were close to panic.

Beth's shaky hand was hovering over certain highly refined products, she whispered, "I'll bring out the sugar."

"No, it's too early" I said. "They'll become hyperglycemic on us here; the whole house could go up."

"Ok, we bring forward pass the parcel."

Our eyes met meaningfully, we knew we were taking a reckless gamble. If we had any more setbacks, we were facing the ugly prospect of 20 minutes or more at the end of the party without a major distraction. This was dangerous stuff. We rolled the dice and prayed.

Beth was the parcel mistress and she knew she was on her own. If things got out of hand I would be too far away to help, for my mission was to hide prizes in the backyard for our *coup de grace*, "The Pirate Treasure Hunt."

Mission accomplished, I slipped back inside the house and sensed immediately that something had gone dreadfully wrong. I wasn't being psychic. I could hear Beth loudly saying, "Ok, Daniel will do this last round and he WON'T LOOK so keep passing the parcel, remember just KEEP PASSING THE PARCEL!"

Pass the parcel had degenerated into total anarchy, some of the children had lied on their resumes - they had not played the game before and they had quickly worked out that passing the parcel was in fact a losing strategy. Strike two - we released the sugar demon.

Sam wasn't in the therapist's couch yet but we were tottering on the razor's edge. The 'treasure hunt' would deliver us either as heroes or as a psychiatrist's taxi service.

The treasure hunt briefing with the children went well; they were excited. The face paints and bandannas (which apparently sounded a lot like bananas) made us all look like pirates and a few throaty "aaaaargh me hearties" made us sound like pirates too.

We headed to the yard again - but this time we had completed the shoe check. The children had to work out where each of the treasures was hidden from clues that a dying pirate had helpfully scrawled onto a treasure map for me.

I drew each clue on a chalk board. I was relying on my shipmates to decipher the clue, find the treasure and bring it back to the treasure chest. They loved the game and there was much rejoicing.

After they found all the treasure they each got to select one prize from the pirate's chest and unwrap it. There was even more rejoicing. From that point on we had them in the palm of our hand, which was just as well.

They collectively shrugged off a potentially calamitous catering blunder. The pass the parcel mistress had forgotten to put all the cheese and spinach rolls in the oven. So what? They happily pigged out on the lollies, crackers, chips and dips instead - no problem.

The cake cutting ceremony went without a hitch although my sneaking suspicion that Sam didn't actually make a wish **before** he blew out the candle was verified later.

As I was tucking him into bed I assured him, "Look, I'm sure they cut a little slack for five year olds at their first big party, man, as long as the candles were still smokin' when you made the wish, that wish is a gimme."

So the party was a huge success, we even went over time and we all enjoyed ourselves - now, only thirteen years to prepare for his 18th birthday party. We better get cracking!

3

The Naming

And so it was that a beautiful, healthy, baby girl was born unto Beth and Daniel and there was much rejoicing. Soon after the birth an angel appeared bearing a name for the little one. Surprisingly, before that angel departed, another angel showed up bearing a different name and then another angel materialized and another and another and another. Twelve angels appeared that night, all with different names.

Now, you wouldn't think that angels would be overly competitive but I tell you it was utter chaos. Each angel was loudly proclaiming that their name was the proper name for the child. There was pushing, bending of wings, plucking of feathers, crushing of halos, pinching and sad to say there was a biter as well. By the time order was restored four yellow cards had been given out, one red card and one of the angels was actually sent off to the 'other place' (we crossed Jezebel off the list straight away).

Apparently there had been a bit of a mix up 'upstairs,' something to do with a bug in the main naming baby girls computer. I couldn't follow how the foul up had occurred. Anyway, we told the Angels that we were very flattered that they had all come down and that we were actually quite exhausted by the birth so we wouldn't be staying up to party but that if they wanted to, they were welcome to stay for a while and could the last angel up please turn off the lights and leave us the lottery numbers for next week.

Well, they stayed for a while, played some cards, drank some of my beers and left an alphabetical naming list on the table. No lottery numbers which was a bit disappointing.

When we woke up the next morning, instead of just one name for our baby girl we had eleven that we both liked but none that we both liked at the same time. Meanwhile our son Samuel was calling his new sister Veronica Bean Bag. He told his pre-school teachers that that was her name so when I went to pick him up I was given a *very* funny look. "You named your child *Veronica Bean Bag*?"

Let's rewind a little here. I was working on my computer one night when Beth swayed in holding her very pregnant belly and suggested it would be a very good idea *not* to have a late night. One look into her eyes and I powered down and then turned off the computer.

Contractions started soon afterwards and our baby girl delivered herself in our home after two and a half hours of labor. Her entrance into this world was heralded by the sound of a friend playing a didgeridoo. She is a very independent, Aussie girl. She must have heard our midwives car pull up outside the house because one minute she was crowning and 2 pushes later she came gushing out with all her waters.

I am officially only credited with an assist as she came gushing out so quickly that all I could do was direct her onto Beth's waiting hands. Beth added another 7 lbs catch to her birthing stats.

The midwives' timing was perfect as they arrived just in time to do all the postnatal checks and help get our girl suckling properly.

I had woken Samuel up about 15 minutes before his sister was born so he could be there for her birth. Shortly after she was born Samuel asked, "Can we call her Veronica?"

I don't know where that name came from. We said that we would have a family conference to decide her name but that it was very unlikely to be Veronica. A short while later he asked, "Can we call her Bean Bag?"

I think I know where that one came from. After the birth, Beth was resting in our bean bag breast feeding our brand new baby. All Samuel probably heard was, "Samuel, get off the <u>bean bags</u>!" "Samuel, leave the <u>bean bags</u> alone," "Samuel, don't jump on the <u>bean bags</u>!"

He was great and just wanted to kiss his little sister but the bean bag kept shifting every time he moved. Sam wasn't interested in going back to sleep, I mean it was only 3:30 A.M., he wasn't tired - we all were.

All parents think that their babies are beautiful. Any evidence to the contrary like scrawny chicken legs or a head that is slightly squished by passage through the birth canal is ignored and this is the way it should be. Our new baby girl, because she came out so quickly with her waters protecting her head, came out perfectly (OK, so she had scrawny chicken legs). She was and is gorgeous.

The naming thing had us stumped for weeks. It wasn't our fault that we had too many pretty names that weren't quite right or sounded ok but would get hacked by the time honoured Australian habit of shortening even one syllable names and then you know there was a middle name that had to go with the first name and barring deed poll she would have this name for the rest of her life so we wanted one that fitted her!

Five weeks and bucket loads of pressure from family and friends later, we left the seven baby name books at home and went out for a coffee with our eleven name 'short' list.

Lo and behold, after a particularly strong long black, the missing piece of the puzzle, her middle name, Cheyenne turned up. Once we had Cheyenne it was a breeze for us to decide on her first name, Aelysha. Whew!! The naming was harder than the birth, well, harder for me anyway.

Now if one of those Angels had been content with bringing a middle name instead of fighting over first name rights we would have had our baby girl, named a lot quicker.

<u>Authors note</u>: It did actually take us about six weeks to name Aelysha and we are all very happy that we waited until her name found her. There is a lot of social pressure to name a baby quickly. Take your time, if you are struggling, find out how long you 'officially' actually have.

Samuel was named very quickly. I had teased Beth that if our first child was born on my birthday and was a boy, we would name him after me, Daniel. Ok, I was a little serious. The best teases do have a grain of truth but the thought of Daniel Junior quickly put me off and Samuel was wisely born a few days after my birthday. There were also lots of Angels present at Sam's birth.

Remember Y2K? This was written just after that non-event.

4

Black Five

"Dad? Dad! Are you AWAKE yet? DAAAAD?"

I jolted awake to find my 4-year-old son kneeling on my chest, staring at me intently. His nose was touching mine. His blue eyes didn't blink. My wildly dilated panicking pupils tried to drop a protective eye lashes but small fingers immediately pulled my eye lid open again. He still didn't blink.

"DAD? Do you remember what today is?"

"Ummmm… Saturday? My day of rest. My sleep in day?" I asked hopefully.

"Nooooo, today is the day you promised me we would make my rocket, remember?"

Technically I didn't remember though I vaguely recalled making a distracted grunt which may have been construed as conciliatory, but it was hardly a promise, it wasn't even a maybe. The grunt had only been elicited after I had endured a prolonged and a highly premeditated nagging campaign.

Surely a mere murmur made under duress doesn't count? Your Honor, I was preoccupied and therefore I wasn't parentally compos mentis. The law was on my side, and I had every right to just fluff my pillow, roll over and slip back into delicious sleep. Good Lord I was tempted but I made the mistake of looking into those unblinking blue orbs, at the hope and excitement that was shining there – and he had me.

I lifted Sam off my chest and took my first breath of the morning as I glibly rep-lied (emphasis on the lied bit), "Of course I remember, a promise is a promise, right?"

I repeated this several times, more for my benefit than Sam's as I desperately hoped that one day it would work in my favour.

"Let's go, buddy."

I turned to my apparently still sleeping spouse and said in my most seductive voice, "Honey, coming to help us build a rocket?"

My spouse opened one eye and smirked. It was definitely a smirk. "No, thank you. I'll keep the bed warm for us both. Rockets definitely sound like a father and son thing. Thanks for asking, hon."

"Now… are you sure?"

"Daaad, come on, stop nagging mum, we've got a busy day." Me? A nag? Referee!

We kept our clandestine rocket factory under the house. After a hurried breakfast Sam and I arrived at the work site and went through the checklist provided by the stationary industrial complex. Cardboard moving boxes; check, sticky tape; check, masking tape; check, scissors and knife; check, paint; check, aluminum foil & cake tins; check, toilet rolls; check, snacks; check, esky; check; vacuum cleaner? No check. It shouldn't have been on the list.

"Sam? What do we need the vacuum cleaner for?"

He rolled his eyes. It was so hard to get quality workers. In a condescending tone he told me: "Propulsion Dad." Obvious, really. I didn't ask what the broom was for. I knew from previous experience that it was not for sweeping.

Our daunting task was to build a two-man rocket that would take us comfortably to wherever we dared to imagine. When I say comfortably, I meant comfortable for Sam to sit in.

To make a rocket that I could climb into would have required either much larger boxes or for me to suddenly become a yoga master. The latter was never going to happen so we settled for a design where I could get my chest and shoulders in my part of the cockpit but my legs were allowed to be outside. Obviously they were sprayed with an ingenious and invisible layer of Insul-legs 2000 which would protect them during flight and re-entry. The clear benefit of me having my legs out was that it would make it easier to walk on the moon. Try and keep up.

It was thirsty work that required frequent juice and snack breaks. We had a blueprint to guide us which was less of a print and more of a blue crayon drawing. All modifications to our original design were carefully marked in orange wax-based ink (crayon) so that they would be preserved for the benefit of future generations. It was awesome to surrender to the project, to be guided and inspired by Sam's vision. Maybe NASA should employ a few 4-year-old consultants?

By lunchtime we had sweated, sawed, glued, taped and cut cardboard until I was seeing brown. Sam explained to me that it had to be all brown at first because it needed to be rust proof. OK.

We had successfully constructed a two-compartment command module which was roughly and actually the size of two large moving boxes. It sat on top of the first and second stage rockets which were all underground and not visible to the uninitiated which included snoopy council inspectors. We agreed that it would be much safer for the neighbours if we used the underground launch pad which was one of the features that had attracted us to the house in the first place.

In case of a mishap our command modules were separate but we had installed a large sliding panel in between. Our controls consisted of various jar lids, bottle tops and foil all carefully calibrated using black texta with twigs as needles. On top of the command module sat our streamlined nose cone with the broom handle jutting proudly out of the middle while the disconnected broom head hid lamely under a pile of scraps. The vacuum cleaner was installed at the back of our command modules to provide extra boost for lift off.

We had discussed whether we were going to need a lunar lander. It took us an entire cup of hot chocolate to exhaustively sift through our only option. We decided that with a few tweaks we could make our command module clever enough to do landings as well as fly in space. No disrespect to NASA but we did have extra strength aluminum foil at our disposal.

The not so heavy lifting done, I went out and left Sam to add the finishing touches prior to our maiden voyage.

When I got back a few hours later Sam excitedly grabbed me and took me to see our completed spaceship. He had been very busy in my absence, and I was pleasantly stunned. With Beth's help, he had found some black paint, as black as space, Sam proudly explained and in the middle of the command module was a large white circle with a black five in the middle of it. 'Black Five' now also had an old TV antenna on the nose cone so we could watch cartoons when space got boring and several additional external engineering enhancements.

It was getting late in the day and despite the fact that some of the paint was still wet, we, or rather Sam, felt that there was enough light for a quick flight to the moon which would also help the paint dry.

The vacuum cleaner engine was plugged in and turned on. The whole ship was vibrating as we went through our final prelaunch check list. All systems were go. We shook hands and slid the partition between compartments shut. We would not reopen the panel until we were in lower Earth orbit or until we shared a snack, whichever came first.

10,9,8,7,6,5,4,3,2,1… BLAST OFF

5

Legal Eaglets

I want them. I desperately want them because if I ever have a tough legal battle, they have to be on my side no matter how much they cost. They are legal geniuses, patient, thorough and razor sharp. They miss nothing.

I don't know who they are, but they must be incredibly gifted. They are the ones who teach toddlers and young children the finer points of law. You know what I'm frothing about; you've seen their precocious prodigies: young 'Legal Eaglets' strutting their stuff, some still in nappies, smiling, laughing and forever poised to ruthlessly exploit the tiniest loophole in parental communication.

My first devastating defeat was "The Ball vs Dad, Lounge Room, 1998."

After playing with my young son Sam all morning I was feeling pooped and called a 5-minute daddy time-out so I could peruse some of the weekend newspaper. The prosecution maintains that the act of spreading the paper on the floor to facilitate reading constituted an unconscionable and irresistible temptation to the defendant.

I defend my actions by maintaining that as the Supreme Ultimate Commander of my castle (reporting directly to my beautiful wife, of course) that it was my inalienable right to sprawl.

My three-year-old was thankfully oblivious to all the dramas, wars, sales and sport that I was trying to read up on just in case I happened to have a conversation with an adult sometime in the next week or three.

Apparently, the ball rolled of its own volition across the paper. Sam, of course, had to retrieve the ball which meant diving on the broadsheet. A window he is not.

"Sam, get off the paper, please!"

The ball, when questioned, simply stated that it couldn't remember anything about the incident at all. Sam claims that the scissors he was playing with could not possibly have intimidated the witness.

Another request for reading space was denied because the ball started wrestling with Sam before he could take it away. I was exasperated but I remained doggedly optimistic about catching up on the news.

After a few more failed attempts at requesting co-operation, I achieved my primary objective by physically rolling him off the paper. Now where was I? Bill Clinton not having sex with Monica Lewinsky, no, that was the last time I read the paper. George Bush apologising for lying to the world, no, but I'd like to read that…

The ball bounced off the wall and then landed on the paper followed quickly by a pair of little bare feet. "Let's play some ball, Dad. You know you want to."

"Sam, I am trying to have just 5 minutes to read the newspaper! So please move so I can read it!"

I was pleading, nay, whining, okay I was begging and just about to launch 'Thomas the Tank Engine' as a boy specific multi-media anesthetic into the video player.

Surprisingly, shockingly, Sam moved off the paper and then he conceded without breaking me, "Ok, Dad, I guess that stupid paper is more important than your own son."

I looked up and saw 'it,' the hunched look of utter devastation that boys do so well. His head was down and his movements were slow and stilted, as though he had lost the will to live or at least to annoy me. A dagger went through my heart – buuuut, it was a small dagger and I had a clear paper. My will was strong that day, my friend.

I think I managed to turn a page before it started.

Thump, thump, thump, thump.

"Sam! Stop throwing the ball against the wall!" The end result of my demand as measured by the behavioural modification co-efficient was exactly zero.

Thump, thump, thump, thump.

I was now effectively trapped in no-dad's land. I had to decide how badly I wanted to catch up on all the terrible things that were happening in the world. I could ignore the ball on the wall and pretend that I had said nothing, or I had to engage in a follow-up action that would require me to get up and forget about the paper for another month or two.

Neither option was very attractive, so I chose the middle path. I stayed put, manically flipping pages. My skim reading became blur glancing as I prepared to deploy 'The Daddy Voice.' I upped my volume to two thirds maximum, dropped it an octave deeper and added another exclamation mark for good luck.

"Samuel!! Stop throwing the ball against the wall!!"

The behavioural modification co-efficient rocketed to minus 3.

THUMP, THUMP, THUMP, THUMP.

That middle path might have worked for Buddha but then Buddha didn't actually bring up his kids, did he? I got up and snatched the ball away from Sam. The resulting tantrum was about 8 out of 10 – sure there were tears and gnashing of teeth and frequent agitated attempts to grab the ball back, but it was really lacking the hysteria that is the hallmark of the truly great tantrums. He was playing well inside himself on this occasion which, frankly, I was fine with.

I was reasonable, I was fair, and I found myself totally out flanked. "Samuel, I told you twice to stop throwing the ball against the wall and you didn't, so now I'm putting it away."

What could be fairer than that?

"Buuut Daaaad, I didn't hear you because the ball was bouncing off the wall." Oh, please. That was rather original. Distracted I committed a fatal blunder, I relented.

"Ok, you can have the ball back as long as you promise not to throw it against the wall? Promise?"

The "yes" was purely rhetorical; I had made it so easy for Sam that it secured a total lack of commitment on his behalf: Another rookie mistake by me.

After bolting back to the paper, I believed for nearly a nanosecond that, despite my lack of experience, I might have somehow created a few minutes of 'me' time. I was poised to pat myself on the back when I heard it.

Tap, tap, tap, tap, tap, tap.

In an instant I was up and towering over the source of the sound, "Samuel, you promised not to throw the ball against the wall!" I was losing the plot by this stage.

"But Daaaad, I'm not throwing it, I'm pushing it."

That is why I want to know who trains these confident post nappy-clad barristers. Who teaches them the fine distinction between a throw and a push? I am convinced that they are fully briefed before they are born.

Children gleefully take advantage of every gap in our communication. On another occasion we had told Sam to stop hitting his sister. Sudden crying brought us outside on the run, "But I didn't hit her… I pinched her."

One of my particular favorites, which was often combined with genuine surprise was, "Oh, you wanted me to pick up the toys NOW?" There are more, many more examples.

So exactly how far away from a wall does a push become a throw? Answer me that and while you're at it, find me the solicitors that train these kids because if I ever need legal assistance, I want them on my side.

P.S. We had a great game of ball.

6

I said "Housework not Hogwarts"

I was afraid that if I uttered the words, "Please help with the housework" one more time that I would etch a groove in my vocal cords so deep that my speech would be forever limited to this totally ineffectual plee. My vision was blurring, and my palms were sweaty. I was close to snapping. The house was an absolute tip, and we had friends coming over in an hour and I wanted the house tidy.

Finally, sensing my impending loss of control as I suddenly loomed over him; my son calmly looked up from his Gameboy and in a detached voice said "Oh, I thought you wanted help with Hogwarts? I thought that that was weird."

I have to declare that I loved the Harry Potter books, and I enjoyed reading them to my children but maybe, just maybe, J.K. could have restricted the House Elf's duties to cooking? Would it be so terrible if the students of Hogwarts had had to clean up after themselves? Or, horror of horror, actually do the washing up? Is it only me or do house elves sound suspiciously like parents?

As far as I know, all parents are muggles. Oh for a spell that will swiftly cook a healthy nutritious supper for hungry whining kids at the end of a long day. Oh for a cleaning spell, any cleaning spell.

After I finished reading Sam the fourth or fifth book of the Harry Potter series, all of our brooms mysteriously disappeared. When they reappeared, they had had their handles sawn down to hobbit size and somewhat ominously we discovered occult words written on them in bold black texta. The words sent a chill down my spine: 'Nimbus 2003.' It could only mean one thing – our children had been playing Quidditch behind our backs.

For a short while after the brooms were modified, whenever we went down to the beach, Sam and Aelysha would tie tea towels around their necks and mount their Nimbus 2003's. On my signal, they would kick off and start 'flying' around on the sand.

Several green tennis balls with writing on them were prepared for me. A large 'Q' for Quaffle, 'B' for Bludger and of course 'S' for the Snitch. As I threw each tennis ball I had to shout out what it was. Obviously, they had to dodge the Bludgers, and try to catch the Golden Snitch as well as any of the Quaffles.

Only an *Imperius Curse* could have made me throw the snitch up in a high lob and then pelt bludgers at them while they were looking up. If they weren't so quick, and if I was a better shot I'm sure I could have tagged one of them.

Unfortunately, they maintain that only an *Imperius Curse* could have made them play 'hit Dad in the head with the Bludgers when he isn't looking' – a game I strongly discouraged.

If only a tiny, tiny, tiny portion of Sam and Aelysha's enthusiasm for the Quidditch broom could have been transformed into enthusiasm for using a broom for its designed purpose then I would stop nagging them, really, I would.

As I stooped over to do the sweeping with our mini-broom I reflected that the brush only truly meets the floor when cleaning. I tried to impart this pearl of home tidiness wisdom to my off-spring but to no avail.

They seem totally immune to all the spells that Beth and I cast at them. Neither *'puttoysawaynowum'* nor *'cleantheroomium'* have any effect. The children seem able to deflect our spells by casting counter jinxes of 'Temporary Deafness' and 'Adult Vision Deficit Disorder.'

Whilst the most surreptitious rustling of a chip packet is enough to restore full auditory functioning the 'Adult Vision Deficit Disorder' jinx is much harder to dispel. A room awash in play detritus and flotsam: toys, books, paper and quite often local vegetation (food for Aelysha's plastic horses) can somehow appear tidy – to them. We wearily explain that when we say that everything has its place we do not mean that everything's place is on the floor < sigh >.

I remember doing a lot more cleaning up when I was a kid and it frustrates me that my own children help so little around the house. I shared these memories with my Dad. At first, he just looked blankly at me and then, when he worked out that I was actually serious, he just started laughing, hysterically. A week later he was still laughing so maybe my memory is being a tad selective. The mind is a funny place.

We know that each time we tidy up for them we are making a bit of a rod for our own backs BUT it is so much quicker to tidy things up without the 'help' of little ones

AND they are so much bigger now and capable of great and so far untapped levels of orderliness.

Those magical words, "What can I do to help?" do echo around our house but at the oddest of times like just after the washing up is finished or just after all the groceries have been carried in, but at least we hear them.

I'm thinking I will put a Bedroom Hazard Sign on Sam's door with an arrow that will point to a colour that represents the level of the room's tidiness or lack thereof and an associated consequence. When Sam's room is in the red it will trigger a total Gameboy ban until the level of chaos is reduced. It might just work, though I suspect that there is no adhesive strong enough to keep such a sign on his door for long.

I disagree with J.K. on one other point; I believe that there are no muggle children. All children are inherently magical and it is our job as parents to create our own mini-Hogwarts where we nurture and keep the magic alive for as long as possible without being reduced to house elf status.

If a slightly messier house means happier children and a happier spouse it actually seems a good trade to me. What good is having a kitchen floor so spotless that you could eat off it if you don't plan to eat off it?

If I am really honest, messiness for my adolescent years was a personal code of honour, but the kids don't know about that… unless a certain Uncle has been telling stories again? Cripes, got to go.

P.S. I still want to see 'Harry Potter and the Chamber of Dirty Dishes.'

7

When Kissing Hurts Better Stops

I had one of those 'ah hah' moments recently when my five-year-old daughter fell over and grazed her knee. I picked her little sobbing body up and wrapped my big daddy arms around her and just held her on my lap until she stopped crying.

I kissed her cheeks and then we inspected the injury together. I asked her if she wanted me to kiss it better. With teary eyes, she nodded a serious 'yes.' I paused for a couple of seconds to give the moment the gravitas that it deserved and to summon the super healing power that all parents are vested with. Gently, tenderly, I kissed the hurt away.

It was one of those prized parenting moments that we can have, a moment of innocence and tenderness, of connection. Aelysha then pointed out a little scar on her knee that looked like a tree and asked me to kiss that too.

I did and 'accidentally' tickled her. She giggled and laughed. I kissed her again and she scampered off my lap straight into a new adventure and I was just struck with melancholy at how fleeting our time with these precious little human beings is.

She was growing up so fast, how much longer would I be able lift her up so easily, wrap her in my arms and kiss the hurts away? I was very present to my love for her and what fabulous teachers my children have been.

As I swung myself back into the 'real' world I smashed my knee into one of the drawers on my desk and let out a not so muffled curse. There have been days when I would have let something like that spoil an entire priceless day.

I knew what I 'kneeded' to do, so I hobbled to the door of my study and yelled, "Aelysha, I hurt my knee, will you come and kiss it better?"

From far away I heard a tiny voice, "I'm playing with my toy horses, kiss it yourself."

When I finished laughing, the pain was gone.

Author's Note: So far, this special parental superpower has not made it into a Marvel comic, and it never should.

8

The Boy Who Punched the Sky

"Once upon a time there was a very brave village. The people there were not afraid of anything. They put monsters in every closet, crocodiles in the creeks and piranhas in their ponds. Instead of a footpath the villagers used tightropes strung between the houses.

The village had grown to be so, well, unusually courageous because of a silly, innocent mistake. The word 'afraid' was missing from the village dictionary, so no one in the village actually knew how to be 'afraid.' Their dictionary did have the word 'concerned' though and there was one tiny little thing that they were very, very, very 'concerned' about. They were 'concerned' that the sky might one day fall on their heads.

In this beautiful and bizarre village there lived a little boy, Calvin, who loved to punch. I mean Calvin really, really loved to punch. He punched everything, from morning till after lunch.

Calvin punched the cat (who scratched him), the dog (who bit him), the budgie (who pooped on him) and even the crocodile (who just missed him). When Calvin had nothing else to punch, he punched himself.

Punching, as all of you would know, will nearly always get you into big, big trouble. Calvin was in trouble so much that he spent most of his time in his bedroom, punching his shadow, his pillows, the bed and his poor battered ted.

The villagers were all very upset and annoyed with Calvin's constant punching. Asking Calvin to stop punching didn't work. Telling Calvin to stop punching didn't work. Bribing Calvin to stop punching didn't work. Begging Calvin to stop punching didn't work and punishing Calvin for punching didn't work.

No matter what they tried, Calvin would always give the same response, "But I have to practice my punching, I was born to punch, I just know it," he would say.

Finally, all the punched parents, punched children and punched pets of the village had a meeting. They all agreed that they really liked Calvin, but they had finally had enough. Calvin was issued with an ultimatum; he had one week to stop punching or else he would have to leave the village. Calvin's mum was very sad; she would miss Calvin.

The sky all that fateful week was stormy and dark and full of bright cracks (lightning). It sounded like the sky was having a lot of trouble staying up. The villagers were very, very 'concerned' about the sky falling so they stayed indoors. Calvin, on the other hand, was punching everything he could reach in his last week.

Despite the dark sky full of cracks, the whole village came out to wave Calvin good-bye. There were many tears, mostly from sore bruised arms. Calvin's mum gave him one last big hug and Calvin gave her one last, affectionate little bop on the nose. He took a deep breath and bravely waved farewell. He knew that if he wanted to keep punching, he would have to go away. So be it. He turned his back and started walking slowly away.

After taking just a few steps, Calvin turned to wave a final, final goodbye to his childhood village. A tear snuck out and ran down his cheek. With a loud sigh, Calvin turned to leave, forever.

Suddenly, the sky gave an almighty boom and actually, really, it fell right on top of everyone's heads, squishing them to the ground. The very thing that they had been so concerned about was happening.

Only Calvin knew what to do. He rolled onto his back, and he just started punching and punching and punching. Calvin kept punching until he punched that ol' sky right back up where it belonged. The villagers were overjoyed. With Calvin around they never had to be 'concerned' about the sky falling on their heads ever again.

The village celebrated and put on a feast for Calvin where they presented him with a pair of very soft boxing gloves. Every house put a punching bag next to their mailbox and they all lived bruised but happily ever after."

"So Mum, that's why I hit my sister, I'm like Calvin. I was born to punch. I just know it."

"Samuel, hitting doesn't solve anything. You have to use your words. Now apologise to your sister and no hitting! Understand?"

"Buuuut Muuuum."

"Samuel!"

"Ok, sorry for punching you, Aelysha."

"That's Ok, Sam."

"And Samuel?"

"Yeeees, Mum."

"I have a new ending for your story."

"At the village celebration, where Calvin ate a whole wild boar all by himself, his wise, beautiful mother announced that she had taught Calvin how to use his words and say how he was feeling instead of punching. From that day forth, the only thing Calvin ever punched was the sky. There was even more rejoicing, and they all lived unbruised and happily ever after."

<u>Authors note:</u> This story was inspired by a few words written on a Christmas card to Sam by one of his friends. All I remember was that there was something written in it about 'punching the sky. I took it from there.

Before 'Picture Books' for children were ever printed there were stories. The stories were told without any pictures to draw the images in the child's head for them. The child had to rely on their imagination. I like this story, and it would also make a great picture book ☺

9

I Love You Like a Rock

Every family that has two children has a first born and a second born child. Kind of basic, one plus one stuff really, except that with children, adding a second child does not just double the workload, does it? Oh no, it is like adding another order of magnitude of effort and it adds other challenges as well that even the most complex mathematics will never address.

On the plus side, when the second baby comes along, you are already a veteran parent, so you almost know what you are doing, some of the time. But no matter how many stripes you have from the first child campaign you have not experienced siblings fighting, teasing, hitting, biting or scratching each other, at least, not since you were a child yourself.

There is nothing quite so exhausting for a parent as two children bickering with each other. "She was in the front the last time!" "He got a micro-milli-nannogram more chocolate than I did."

"Daaaaad, he gave me a really funny look," and all this just as a prelude to full body sibling combat!

As a second child myself, I think the first born has a really tough job. They have to break in the parents. They have to take the brunt of their inexperience; they have to teach the parents to chill out a bit so they don't pop a vein. As number two, you have the luxury of sitting back and going, "Oh… Ok, so he got in big trouble for doing that so I either don't do it or I do it and blame him for it, cool. Next lesson please."

In their wonderful book '*Siblings without Rivalry*,' Adele Faber and Elaine Mazlish compare how a first child might feel when a second child shows up to how a wife might feel if her husband brought home a second wife. "Honey, I love you so very much that I've brought another wife home." Youch!

Whilst the older child loves the new baby there is no doubt that at times the green monster of "you love them more than me" will rear its ugly head. It seems, at times, that no amount of reassurance will kill this vampire of self-esteem.

In mid-rivalry, children start to measure everything in quanta of blood, I mean, love. "You gave her an extra hug, see, I know you love her more than me."

"No, I love you totally as you, as my first born. I can love no one else the way I love you and you have a place in my heart that is just for you." This is the truth but often there is no listening, no receptivity for this logic by the child.

"Yeah, but that place is now halved, isn't it? Because SHE came along."

Aaaaagh! Maybe it was easier when kids were seen but not heard? But ignorance of issues doesn't make them go away and if ignorance is bliss wouldn't there be a lot more happy people in the world today?

I have agonized over this 'you love her more than me' dilemma which only gets verbalised at times of high emotion. I thought that I had finally cracked a cure one day and I wanted to share my thinking with Sam. First though, I had to get his attention, so I placed my face between the Gameboy screen and his body. It worked.

"Sam, I love you like a rock," I said.

"Right, thanks Dad, now can you just move your head a little?"

"Nope, we're going outside."

Having successfully achieved *Gameboy interuptus* I led my reluctant helper into the great unplugged outdoors. I must have been looking a little evangelical because Sam asked me a couple times if we really needed to do this. "I know you love me, so can I just go play Gameboy now?"

I was not to be swayed. We walked to a nearby open field. "Sam, you are a rock."

"Right and you're a rock too Dad, now can I go?" I grabbed his hand and turned him to face me.

"Find me a big rock that is you, while I dig a hole." Shaking his head so hard I worried it might fall off, Sam wandered off. I had just put the shovel down when he returned with a good sized rock. I could see it was heavy.

"Right! Now, who are you?"

"I'm this rock… see ya." And with this response he dropped the stone and started to scamper off.

"No, Sam, stop; play with me on this, it's important. Now, look all around you."

Sam looked. I looked. "Sam, consider that my heart, my love, is like the earth, way bigger than this large open field. Now, put yourself into my heart." I pointed helpfully at the rock.

He dropped the rock into the hole I had dug. Together we covered the rock with about a meter of fresh earth.

"OK, now where are you?" I asked Sam.

"Suffocating."

I laughed. "You are buried," I corrected.

"OK, I'm buried in your heart."

"Excellent, how does it feel?"

"Dirty," he said with a grin.

"Sam, close your eyes for a second, how does it really feel to be wrapped permanently in my love?"

Sam took a second before he responded, "Good… very good."

"Excellent! Now can you see that you have a place in my heart that is totally unique to you, that nobody can take away."

Sam shook his head no.

"It will help if you open your eyes." With a cheeky smile, Sam opened his eyes and nodded his head in affirmation.

"Sam, how much room is there in my heart for other people?"

"Heaps, big heaps."

"Exactly, in fact, everyone has the capacity to love everyone else."

"Yeah, right, then why don't they?"

"How easy would it be to let people into your heart if there was a layer of concrete on the surface?"

"Nothing would get in," Sam observed.

"Precisely, and the concrete that covers people's hearts is made up of fear and old hurts both real and imagined. Some people put a fresh layer of cement on every day. For some lucky people things happen that smash the layers of concrete into smithereens."

"Like what?" Sam asked.

"Like falling so madly, deeply in love that there is no concrete thick enough that can keep a love like that out of someone's heart."

Sam was silent for a moment. "Wow, that sounds cool… and have you had that happen?"

"Yes, I've been very lucky. You see sometimes that kind of love happens like with your Mom and me and sometimes if we are really, really lucky and we create the right space we can be blasted wide open by bunker busting babies. Babies' hearts are totally open, they are love. You see, for me, no concrete survived the moment when I first held you in my arms. I had no idea that would happen. In that moment, my heart was totally open, like this field."

Sam looked deeply into my eyes and he knew that this was so. It was an amazing moment, I saw the fang marks in his neck start to heal and the whole world stood still. "I love you like a rock too, Dad. Thanks."

After the longest of hugs, I asked Sam if he would choose a rock that was his sister so I could show him that my love for her did not take away or diminish in any way the love that I had for him.

A short while later he returned. He was looking very pleased with himself. I asked him to show me what he was holding behind his back.

"Sam, I said a rock, not a potato!"

10

The Cuddle Bank

What would you build to hold your most precious things, items that are priceless, irreplaceable? Are you thinking of a bank or a safe? What if I told you that your goal was to design a structure that holds Love? Love captured in a series of very special moments?

A normal bank holds money, maybe some safe deposit boxes and these days, lots of electrons. Banks are normally built to be functional, perhaps imposing, planned to maximise profit, keep the vault secure and make a few people rich.

A 'Cuddle Bank' is a unique mind space designed to hold exquisite and fleeting experiences as memories. It has to be beautiful. It is open 24/7 for deposits and for withdrawals but unlike a financial bank, the more times you take memories out, the richer your account gets. Another feature of the Cuddle Bank is that every account is a joint account. It operates on a double entry system: for every deposit a parent makes, there is also a corresponding deposit in a child's account.

The Cuddle Bank can cope with a flood of affection-rich deposits and as our children get older the rate at which deposits are made slows and once our children leave home, the deposits become sporadic, at best. The ebbs and flows are intrinsic to the nature of the Cuddle banking system and reflect the natural evolution of the relationship between parents and children.

As a Dad, I was never told about the importance of creating a Cuddle Bank. I just started doing it. I created an account and started making deposits from the moment I held my new born babies. I could have stopped kissing them on their downy little heads all the time but I didn't even try. When they were tiny I loved carrying them in a baby sling on my chest and on my back in a back pack when they were bigger. Both devices facilitated me making multiple direct deposits into our cuddle account.

I loved having little arms wrapped around my neck and the memories of a little sleeper resting peacefully in the backpack, head safely on my shoulder are securely stored in our accounts. Sleeping with my baby in my arms, swings, slippery dips, sand castles and wrestling. I loved being both a parent and a climbing frame too, most of the time.

I used to go for runs on the beach, leaving Sam and Aelysha playing with Beth. They would look for me when I was jogging back and when I got close they would come racing up to me as fast as they could with their arms open wide wearing ear to ear grins. I opened up my arms on approach and I would sweep them both up in a big sweaty hug before we went for a swim. Those moments are on one of the many trophy shelves I have installed in my Cuddle Bank.

When I was reading books to Sam he would rest his head on my shoulder, CHING CHING, straight into the Cuddle Bank. Good night kisses, CHING CHING. Home from work hug, CHING CHING. Photo hug, CHING CHING.

I've even banked when Sam and Aelysha gave each other a cuddle. MY BANK, my rules. Photos and videos help keep some of the memories alive.

My Cuddle bank holds a plethora of cuddles, kisses and hugs and as my children have grown up I have come to realise just how important and precious the Cuddle Bank is. The Cuddle Bank promotes connection and happiness and it is a vital counter weight to the pernicious 'Book of Hurts.' The Book of Hurts is a stealer of happiness and it seeds resentment, conflict and misery.

The Book of Hurts is a volume listing all of the real and imaginary slights that have ever happened. It contains entries going back as far as our own childhood. Once opened, this book has a nasty habit of exaggerating problems and creating a vortex that sucks in entries that are unrelated and do not deserve remembering. I try hard to avoid writing in this book and I have even been successful in erasing a few notations. Once an entry is in, it is rarely questioned.

When parenting small children, everything is very immediate – the full nappy needs changing now, child needs food now, child fallen over needs picking up and holding now, put them to bed now and pray that they fall asleep swiftly. When parenting is so urgent and busy there is not much time for self-reflection. The parent gives a lot and it can be exhausting and sometimes frustrating BUT there is also so much coming back from the child in priceless physical contact. Sweet hugs and kisses and 'I love you.'

Most small children are very demonstrative. As they get older, things change. They become more self-conscious and they grow and grow. Lifting them up gets progressively tougher until the time when even giving a little piggy back ride can turn you into a big quivering slab of bacon.

Children grow up and we fall, jump or get pushed off the pedestal that they once put us on. I thought that when my kids became teenagers that my job would be done and I could get back to 'me' time. I can hear some of you laughing. Parenting a teenager is very different from parenting a small child, they still need us but it is, usually, not so immediate, not so obvious.

Teenagers will challenge us, push boundaries and during puberty, parents are advised to buckle up and hold on. When the house undergoes a sudden decompression, and it will, no oxygen masks ever drop from the ceiling but it is always a very good idea to take some deep breaths anyway. I found that between crises, there was plenty of time for self-reflection which could easily turn into self-recrimination. This is a time when the Book of Hurts hungers for attention.

In the adolescent years, in between dodging the odd missile of emotion or grenade of pique the hug tally still grows but slowly and the credits tend to come in as quick isolated contact, rather than as lingering connection. To be fair, they can be big hugs. During one lull, I even banked some 'teen speak' which consisted of a head nod, a positive lifting of the left eyebrow and an upturned lip. My BANK, my rules. It was a pretty special eyebrow lift which had a smile attached.

During challenging times, I like to visit the Cuddle Bank and make a few withdrawals, to remember all the shared love and precious moments. It helps keep the Book of Hurts safely sealed. I think that without enough deposits in the Cuddle Bank, the Book of Hurts can get out of control and this can lead to a lot of disharmony because, you see, the

Book of Hurts fights dirty. It encourages entries made whilst under the influence, under the influence of emotional pain. No 'fairness test' is ever applied. Indeed, exaggeration and fabrication are encouraged by the hurt editor.

What concerns me is that we live in a society where that precious and fleeting time with our children seems to be grist to the mill of increased worker productivity. Is outsourcing child rearing really good for the GDP? No matter how good a childcare worker is they cannot make deposits into the joint parent/child Cuddle account. When parents are suddenly confronted by a large, grunting teenager who has taken over the body of their sweet little boy or girl there may not be enough Cuddle Bank reserves to help manage the Book of Hurts.

The Book of Hurts is not a mandatory dual entry system. A child or adolescent can make deposits that a parent has no idea about and would be completely baffled by and vice versa. A big enough argument or fight can achieve multiple entries though the entries may not be recognizable as having the same origin. All entries in the Book of Hurts are automatically classified as non-fiction, however some prose definitely nudges into the fiction genre and the greater the hurt, the greater the creative license.

Unfortunately, once an entry is made in the Book of Hurts, the story that we tell ourselves about what happened, becomes real. Every time that story is replayed it reinforces the pain and makes it harder and harder to edit or delete the infectious item. Eventually the pain can become so familiar that it is addictive and our powerful need to be right can trump our right to be happy. Thankfully, authentic communication, forgiveness and love can open entries in the Book of Hurts for editing or deletion. My Cuddle Bank is a lifelong shared foundation that makes it easier to create the safe, trusting space required for this to happen.

Time with our children is exquisite. The windows of opportunity for making deposits of special moments is not a constant. There are some who say that shared love and inspiring memories may even last for more than one lifetime. I don't know about that, but I do know that parenting is a long game, that it started before my child's first breath and will continue until my last breath.

My children have grown up so quick. The interest I receive on each deposit made to the Cuddle Bank, my 'Return on Affection,' helps the whole world and reminds me of the following quote by Lloyd de Mause;

"Every abandonment, every betrayal, every hateful act towards children returns tenfold a few decades later upon the historical stage, while every empathetic act that helps a child become what he or she wants to become, every expression of love towards children heals society and moves it in unexpected, wondrous new directions." Lloyd de Mause

I am very happy that I created so much time with my children. Our accounts are full and even when my children have left home, I can still dip into my account and smile.

11

The Power of Please
"Putting the Magic into Magic Words"

Timmy was a delightful little boy. Adults loved him, animals loved him, insects loved him (even spiders) and of course, he had lots of friends. Timmy had a special gift, *he knew magic.*

Timmy could make sweets, books, toys and even a baby sister appear out of thin air. Well, these things didn't really come out of thin air (especially not his sister) but the way that Timmy asked for things made it so easy for people to give them to him that they nearly always did.

Timmy's magic was a secret shared only with his wise Grandmother who was queen of all the witches at 24A Little Barnwick Street East.

You see, on Timmy's fifth birthday, his grandmother gave him a magic word: "The magic word, Timmy, is 'please.' It is a very, very special word. I will also give you a poem which will help you remember it.

For your wants and needs
It's polite to say 'please'

A magic word used well
Has more power than any spell."

As his grandmother finished the poem there was a loud POP and a bright rainbow filled the room. Timmy blinked. In his grandmother's outstretched hand was his 'please,' written on a card, sitting snugly in a jewel encrusted box. Ever since that day, Timmy had used his magic word very well, until…

One dark, dark, morning Timmy woke up feeling a little funny. Not the joke telling kind of funny but the, there's something not quite right sort of funny. Unfortunately, Timmy was hungry, and he forgot all about it as he raced down for breakfast.

At the table Timmy said, "I'm thirsty!" He waited, but nothing happened. How odd.

"Can I have a drink?" Timmy asked. His Mother just kept on making his school lunch. Strange, he thought, maybe she just didn't hear me. Maybe. Being very thirsty, Timmy got up and poured himself a glass of water.

At school, Timmy said to Miss Hollis, "Can I clean the chalk board?"

Eventually Miss Hollis said, "Yes, Mary you may clean the chalk board." But Mary had asked after Timmy. Maybe it was just Mary's turn. That was it. Maybe.

That night, after finishing his supper, Timmy asked, "Can I have some ice cream?" No response. Nothing, just chew, chew, chew from his Dad.

Timmy tried again, louder, "**CAN I HAVE SOME ICE CREAM?!**" At once his Dad got up and took his empty plate into the kitchen.

'Great' thought Timmy, sometimes all it takes is a bit of volume. Timmy yawned. I wonder if it will be strawberry or vanilla? Timmy wondered for quite a while. In fact, Timmy fell asleep at the table, still wondering.

The next morning Timmy woke up and looked outside, 'Oh, oh,' it was another dark, dark morning. At breakfast, Timmy told his Mum, "I'll have bacon today."

After Timmy waited patiently for his bacon he started waiting impatiently for his bacon until finally he whined, "Muuuuum, why aren't you getting me my bacon?"

"Young Timothy" said his mother, in her best lecturing voice, "Have you lost your please?"

Timmy's head snapped up and he dashed to his bedroom. His special box was not where he always kept it. Timmy's Mum was right, he had lost his please.

"Oh, no, no, no." Where was it? "Muuuum! Help me! P- p-p-p-please."

Timmy's Mum was there in an instant "Timmy, what is it? Are you hurt?"

"Look!"

His Mum looked, then shook her head, confused.

Timmy pointed, "It's not there!" he said.

"I'm looking for something that's not there?" asked his Mum. Timmy, on the verge of tears, simply nodded.

"My please, the prince, it's missing," said Timmy finally and a single salty tear trickled down his cheek, "it was in the special jewel encrusted box that Grandma gave me." Timmy recited the poem:

"For your wants and needs
It's polite to say 'please'
A magic word used well
Has more power than any spell."

"I've lost my magic word," said Timmy softly. Another tear snuck out and ran down his face. Timmy's Mum knew just what to do when her little boy was sad. She swept him up into a big, big Mummy hug and held him tight.

Snuggling in his Mother's arms always made Timmy feel better but what was he going to do? Would Grandma ever trust him with more magic? Timmy sighed a huge sigh. "I'll have to tell Grandma the truth." Timmy's little shoulders slumped.

Just then, Lilly, Timmy's baby sister, crawled quickly into the room and plomped herself down. Lilly was so excited she almost wriggled out of her nappy.

Lilly, it seemed, was holding something in her pudgy, sticky little hand. "Preease," she said and she opened her fingers to reveal Timmy's special box.

Timmy was overjoyed. Quickly, but gently, Timmy took the box from Lilly and clutched it tightly to his heart. He opened the box and then he did something that he didn't expect to do.

Timmy gave the box back to his baby sister. "Thank you Lilly, you can keep it. I know now that the Power of Please is always within me. I just have to remember it." As Timmy finished saying this, a strong voice came from behind them.

"For your wants and needs
It's polite to say 'please'
A magic word used well
Has more power than any spell."

Timmy's Grandmother had been quietly watching. Her face was lit up with pride and joy. "Timmy! Timmy! Timmy! I do believe that you are ready for more magic!"

12

Thinking of Thank You
"Putting the Magic into Magic Words"

Timmy's Grandmother arrived at exactly 9:30 AM, just as she had said she would. Timmy loved his Grandma, she was a wise woman, no wonder she was Queen of all the witches at 24A Little Barnwick Street East.

Timmy squirmed with excitement. Maybe today Grandma will trust me with another Magic Word! he thought. But first, they were going to the park, where his favourite swing waited to take him to the clouds. What a great day it was going to be!

At the park, Timmy had the swing all to himself AND Grandma to push him. Brilliant! Timmy was a swing-a-holic, he could swing until his arms nearly fell off but usually there were lots of children waiting for their turn. Not today!

After a while, but well before Timmy's arms fell off, a little girl arrived. Timmy stopped so she could have a turn. Unfortunately, the little girl was wearing a stormy frown. She snatched the swing from Timmy, grunted "Thank you," at the ground and got on.

Timmy looked up at his Grandmother. His eyes were suddenly a bit watery, probably from all that swinging. Why had that little girl been so rude? Timmy felt like his brilliant day had just been spoilt.

"I am thinking of a magic word for you, Timmy. I am thinking of, thank you," Grandma said, looking well pleased with herself.

"You're welcome, Grandma."

"No, Timmy, I mean, 'thank you' *is* the magic word."

"But Grandma, isn't 'thank you,' two words?" asked Timmy.

"You are quite right, Timmy" explained Grandma, "but as far as Magic Words go, 'thank you,' is considered just one magic word."

"This magic word stuff sure is confusing."

Grandma smiled, "Yes, Timmy it is," she continued:

"Saying 'thank you' will show
That your manners you know
A magic word used well
Has more power than any spell"

Grandma had barely finished when a spectacular, foot stomping, breath holding tantrum erupted nearby. Only after the little boy actually turned purple did he finally take a breath.

Using the new air in his lungs, the little boy began to shout, "NO, NO, NO, NO" as loudly as he could, which was surprisingly loud for his size.

Every time he shouted, the boy's mother got crankier and more upset. "It really is time to go. I have to get to work. WE HAVE TO GO NOW, JOHNNY!" she shouted, but it made no difference.

Timmy had seen a lot of tantrums, some of them, in fact had been his very own, but he had never seen a Johnny tantrum before. After finally catching Johnny, his hot, bothered mother carried him, still screaming, from the playground.

As Johnny's Mum struggled past, they heard her say between gritted teeth, "I am never taking you to the park before work ever again!"

"Wow," said Timmy, strangely excited. "I think next time I'm gonna try holding my breath when I ...," Timmy paused as he looked up at his Grandma, "when I... um ... dive into the... um ... swimming pool, yeah."

Grandma rapped her ancient walking stick hard on the ground three times. CRACK. CRACK. CRACK.

"Saying 'thank you' will show
That your manners you know
A magic word used well
Has more power than any spell"

Timmy's head spun, he felt like he was falling backwards, and he was! He was somehow back on the swing and Timmy could see the little girl arrive just like before. Timmy leaned back and kicked his legs as hard as he could but no matter how hard he tried, he kept slowing down. It was as if… as if a slowing spell had been cast on him.

"Grandma!"

As the swing stopped, Grandma whispered, "Be nice, Timmy." The little girl was still wearing her frown but this time she looked Timmy in the eyes and said, "Thank you for stopping."

Timmy saw something behind her frown. "You seem sad," said Timmy.

The girl's frown wavered, and a tear escaped. "My puppy is very sick."

"Oh," said Timmy, "I hope your puppy gets better soon."

As she started to swing she smiled, for the first time that week.

As they walked away, Grandma asked, "How did you feel this time, when she said, 'thank you'?"

Timmy thought for a moment, "It felt good. Looking me in the eyes made me feel like she meant it, like she really appreciated me stopping."

"Saying 'thank you' will show
That your manners you know
A magic word used well
Has more power than any spell"

"So, Grandma, just knowing a magic word isn't enough to make it work, is it? You have to, you know," and Timmy winked at his Grandma (with both eyes) "know how to cast the word, to use it well? Don't you?"

"Timmy, you are so very clever, there is no magic in just saying a word. You have to mean it too."

"Grandma? Can I tell Mum and Dad what I've learned today?" asked an excited Timmy.

"Of course you may, Timmy."

They were now walking past little Johnny. Johnny was holding his mother's hand, looking up at her. "Thank you, Mum, for taking me to the park. I really, really want to stay but I know you have to go to work."

"You're welcome, Johnny. You know, I think we should do this more often."

"This morning was totally sick!" said Johnny.

Grandma, nearly fell over. Timmy helped his Grandma regain her balance and he whispered in her ear, "Totally sick, means really, really good Grandma." Grandma was most relieved and quite confused to hear this.

Later, back at home, Timmy's Dad was staring deeply into Timmy's Mum's eyes. "Honey?" he said, "Thank you. Thank you for everything you do around this house. I realized, after talking with Timmy, that I don't say 'thank you' enough. Thank you."

Timmy's Mum gave his Dad a big hug and just as they started to kiss, Timmy felt his Grandma tap him on the shoulder.

"Let's go out and get an ice cream, Timmy."

Timmy grinned, "That would be totally sick, Grandma."

13

Samuel's Sand

When God was creating heaven and earth and all creatures great and small, I don't think She was living near the beach and pretty sure that She didn't have small children jumping all over her bed.

Don't get me wrong, She did a great job. I mean, fantastic planet, really super though getting a bit shabby around the industrial and heavily populated bits and let's face it, the human body is an engineering marvel, self-healing and what about the whole birth process, eh? Genius, pure genius.

So, I don't mean to be nitpicky because I know way more about nits now than I ever wanted too but, it's just, well, there are so many crevices on a human body where sand can be stored and I am sick of it. The 'squeaky' beaches of fine white quartz sand around Byron Bay are too beautiful to boycott just because of a rash of sand on sheets but it irks me big time when I am trying to fall asleep and it feels like there are entire sand dunes on the sheets.

To try to remedy this situation we have implemented strict sand mitigation procedures but they are just not effective. After a visit to the seaside, despite vociferous protests and regular whining, our children are subjected to a thorough wipe down with a towel before they are allowed to even get into the car. In theory we are all sand free from this point on. In theory.

I am flabbergasted by the sheer volume of clandestine beach granules a kid can successfully carry from the beach into the home. I'm guessing they can hold two to three cotton sheets worth of sand just in their gluteal clefts… their butt cracks. I've never actually checked but I am basing this estimation on the sand levels that have become a semi-permanent feature of our marital bed. Of course, it could just be a clever and effective ploy to stop additional siblings being conceived.

My children are welcome to leave sediments in their own beds but nooo, they would rather give the gift of fine quartz particles to their parents. My theory is that they save their deposits until they start a slow release by bouncing, jumping and somersaulting on our bed. And don't start me on how much sand they can secrete in their pockets and socks. I simply can't go there. I suspect the laws of physics do not extend into the lining of a child's pocket and I can't say I blame physics for that.

I am sick of trying to sleep on sandy sheets, sick, sick, sick of it I tell you. I am so sick of it I'm prepared to ask the big question of God, do we really need to have a gluteal cleft at all? C'mon, answer me that?

There is a teensy possibility that when the sand in my hair and stuck to my scalp dries out that it sprinkles generously onto my pillow which funnels the sand efficiently onto the sheets. Or I can blame the kids and God.

Did I forget to mention that we also have a dog?

14

The Pillock

It is a sunny day. If you were looking for a typi-bloody-cal Aussie backyard barbeque this would be the one you would go to.

The men are all standing around the Barbie drinking beers until the women call Barbie over to help them with the salads. With Barbie gone the men return to the grill which is almost ready to start cooking.

The prawns can't wait to start sizzling: Actually, being dead they don't really give a crap one way or another but in anthropomorphism that isn't the point. You might call a prawn a shrimp but in Australia there are no shrimps, only prawns.

A few young children are sledging each other as they play backyard cricket. The bowler, Trevor, is told by his brother Greg, to try an underarm bowl. Trevor refuses. Kids.

Tristan and Sheila enter the backyard through the side gate. Sheila gives Tristan a peck on the cheek, but Tristan seems distant. Sheila waits for a reaction and when she doesn't get one, she shrugs and joins the women.

Tristan takes a deep breath before he hoists his six pack and walks over to join the menfolk. He is carrying a bottle of red wine.

The owner of the house, Bruce, looks up and watches the couple arrive. Sheila was a new friend of his wife's but what she saw in the pillock she was with he could not see. Bruce couldn't remember his name but that was never a problem.

As Aussie in charge of a barbeque, he had an obligation to extend the customary greeting even if he didn't particularly want to.

"G'day, mate, want a beer?" Bruce extends his right hand as part of the ritual. The resulting handshake is not satisfactory for either man. For Bruce it is just not firm enough and for Tristan it feels like it's the start of an arm wrestle.

Tristan holds up his bottle of wine. Bruce perseveres: "Sure ya don't want a coldie first, mate?" Tristan holds the bottle higher and gives it a little shake.

"Yeah, I'll get ya a beer, as a starter." Bruce walks off towards the fridge. Swampy, aka Tim Marsh, is turning the food on the grill. He puts another prawn on the barbie when he notices Tristan. He can't remember his name.

"Maaaate, how are ya?" Swampy waves a recently skewered headless prawn at Tristan instead of shaking his hand.

"Oh, hi. Swampy isn't it?" Swampy nods confirmation and Tristan continues, "I'm a bit snappy actually, Swampy. Sheila dragged me along to a totally crap movie this morning."

Swampy adds some crushed garlic to the sizzling prawns on the hot plate and nods sagely. "Chic flick huh? Slow, dull, full of deep meaningful looks? An action and adrenalin drought, eh?"

Tristan frowns, "No, actually, lots of violence, big battle scenes, pretty much non-stop action - it sucked."

Swampy is confused and he asks, "Mate, that sounds solid to me. I know you're here with Sheila but ya don't bat for the other team do ya? Not that there's anything wrong with that," he adds hurriedly.

"No way, I just hate the whole fantasy, imaginary Lord of the Rings rubbish."

Bruce has just come back with a can of beer in each hand. Tristan's remark launches him and sends him into a low earth orbit. Gesticulating violently at Tristan, he shouts, "What? What? Are you an idiot? Or insane? You must be a thick head or something. How could you not like Lord of the Rings?"

Tristan doesn't react to Bruce's rage, "I just hate all that magic, hobbity, elvish, dwarf, garbage."

Bruce was speechless; he had never met anyone who hated Lord of the Rings before, so he hadn't bothered to write a speech about it.

He did continue to use the beer in his right hand to emphasise every word of the very limited tirade that he was adlibbing.

In a choked voice he finally manages to confide: "God, I love those films, luv 'em, poor Frodo and… and Sam, what a top mate."

Bruce pauses for a breath before he berates Tristan again; "You are a stupid asshole, wanker, uncultured dick head." A few poorly chosen words hastily thrown together doth not a speech make.

As Bruce is feeling into his tirade his 6'4" bulk is leaning further and further over Tristan. Oblivious, Tristan shrugs his shoulders, "I hate 'em."

Bruce's young son, Jack, is sitting in his little plastic Flintstone's car watching the interaction intently.

Bruce has to have the last word. "Mate, you are seriously a couple of Tim Tams short of a pack. Streuth a brick! I should belt some sense into ya…"

From the women's side of the backyard, Bruce's wife shouts over, "Oi, Bruce. Bruce! Come over here. Sheila's going to be little Jack's new pre-school teacher."

Bruce stops standing over Tristan and thrusts the beer that he has been shaking at him. Tristan points to the other beer, the one that has not been used to punctuate Bruce's poorly constructed points of view.

Bruce looks daggers at Tristan and hands him the beer he wants. "Whatever. Ya freak!"

Bruce walks over to Cheryl. Jack stares at Tristan then pedals over to be with his Dad. Bruce puffs his chest out and congratulates Sheila. As Bruce opens his beer it sprays all over him.

Jack's little friend Jimmy walks over next to Jack. He is innocently holding a ball. Jack is now next to his Dad. He puts the car in gear by lifting his feet up and climbs out.

Jack turns and starts poking Jimmy hard in the chest.

"What Jimmy? What are ya? An idiot? Or a thick head or something? How can you not like The Wiggles? Little Red Car is a classic. You are a freak! Ya hear me, a freak and I'm gonna knock your block right off!"

Jimmy is frightened by Jack. "Jack, I'm not a freak, I just don't like skivvies."

Jack pulls back his arm to deliver a big punch.

Jimmy yells, "Noooooo!"

Bruce is thrashing about in his sleep yelling "Noooooo." Cheryl shakes him vigorously to wake him up.

"Bruce! Bruce! Wake up!"

Finally, Bruce snaps out of it. He is sweating profusely and out of breath.

"Bruce, are you all right?"

Bruce is shaking, he takes a moment to come to his senses. "It was awful. Jack was behaving like a, like ... like... "

Cheryl has just been woken up and is tired and impatient. "Yeeees, out with it Bruce."

Bruce is struggling with a revelation. "He was behaving badly… like... like I behave sometimes."

Cheryl stares at Bruce for a long moment before she turns her back on him and pulls the covers up. The room has become decidedly chilly.

"Bruce, the day I see Jack behaving like a bully, is the day you move out. You might want to have a go bag ready, dear."

Bruce is left sitting up in bed, shoulders slumped, he knows that Cheryl means it and he loves his wife and his boy. It would rip him open if he had to leave.

The next day, at his barbeque Bruce watches in amazement as Tristan and Sheila walk in the side entrance. The feeling of déjà vu puts a shiver up his spine.

Sheila gives Tristan a peck on the cheek. Tristan seems a bit distant. Sheila waits for a reaction and when she doesn't get one, she shrugs and joins the women.

Tristan takes a deep breath. He is well fit. He flexes his six pack in annoyance before he walks over to join the menfolk. He is carrying the same bottle of red wine.

"G'day, Tristan, want a beer?" Bruce extends his right hand as part of the ritual.

Tristan holds up his bottle of wine. Bruce stares at it: Eventually he says, "Sure, I'll get ya a glass." Bruce walks off towards the kitchen.

Swampy is putting another prawn on when he notices Tristan. "Maaaate, how are ya?"

"Oh, hi. Swampy isn't it?" Trevor nods confirmation and Tristan continues, "I'm a bit snappy actually, Trev. Sheila dragged me along to a crap movie this morning."

Swampy adds some crushed garlic to the prawns on the hot plate and nods sagely. "Chic flick huh? Slow, dull, full of deep meaningful looks? An action and adrenalin drought, eh?"

Tristan frowns, "No, actually, lots of violence, big battle scenes, pretty much non-stop action- it sucked."

Swampy is confused and he asks, "Mate, that sounds solid to me."

"No way, I just hate the whole fantasy, fictiony Lord of the Rings rubbish."

Bruce has just come back with a wine glass in one hand. Tristan's remark threatens to launch him into a low earth orbit but he looks over at his son and somehow, he manages to re-enter reason's atmosphere.

After a monumental struggle he manages to squeak out; "God, I love those films, luv 'em. How can you not like them?"

Tristan replies blithely, "I just hate all that hobbity, elvish, dwarf, garbage."

Bruce's three year old son, Jack, is sitting in his little plastic Flintstone's car watching the interaction intently.

Bruce takes a very deep breath. He looks down and sees Jack looking up at him. He takes a very deep breath, "Like I said, I love 'em... but, you're entitled to your opinion."

After a moment of silence where silence is on the pill and doesn't want to get pregnant, Bruce continues, "So you don't like any sci-fi or fantasy movies?"

Tristan shakes his head in the negative as he sips his wine. Bruce persists, "Battlestar Galactica?"

Tristan puts his hand out with his thumb up before he turns it to a thumbs down.

Bruce tries one last time, "Dr. Who? Star Wars?"

Tristan uses his free hand to pinch his nose as he shakes his head, but he is smiling now. Tristan finally throws Bruce a bone, "I think it's because I was bottle fed."

Bruce looks up at Tristan surprised and they laugh together, sharing a moment. Bruce lifts his beer and Tristan his wine glass and they salute one another as they have a drink.

From the other side of the yard Cheryl calls out, "Oi, Bruce. Bruce! Come over here. Sheila's going to be little Jack's new pre-school teacher

Bruce looks back at Tristan as he smiles and scoops little Jack up in his arms. As soon as Bruce can, he takes his wife aside and whispers urgently, "Honey, is it too late to take Jack off the bottle and put him back on the boob?"

Authors note: I had fun writing this and I originally wrote it as a short film script.

15

The Wedgey Snake

The creation myth for wedgies and why there are no snakes in Ireland.

Once upon a time there was a rare and unclassified Irish snake that had an identity crisis and an overbite. The overbite contributed significantly to his character confusion.

Big fangs are common in poisonous snakes, but the fangs always fold neatly within highly elastic mouths. The end of this snake's fangs continued to stick out no matter how hard he tried to retract them. Either his mouth was too small, or his fangs were just too darn big.

Snakes are surprisingly insecure about their dentition. The serpent code is that you never reveal your fangs unless you intend to use them, but it is fine to stick your tongue out at any time.

Unfortunately, all the other snakes thought that the constant fang display was psychological rather than physical. They thought that he was a showoff rather than a one off. The buck toothed snake didn't think he could be less popular with his cold-blooded brethren. How wrong he was.

Despite his long fangs he found out he wasn't venomous. He had tried killing his prey by just giving them a little nip and whilst one vile old rat had conveniently died laughing, all the other prey had run away, bitten but smirking.

Pythons have an ability to partially hypnotise their prey by moving rhythmically before constricting them. He tried this too but as soon as his potential prey caught sight of his overbite, they would begin to giggle which inevitably broke the hypnotic spell and they would wriggle free of his hug of death and scamper safely away.

He had neither family, nor even a genus, and without either of those he would never find his species. He was a hungry and unhappy snake. His unhappiness was cut short, however, when it was replaced with utter misery. Whilst snoozing in the sun he was captured and put in a special animal Zoo.

He was the most popular exhibit in the show but every human that looked inside his cage just pointed and laughed at him no matter how scary he tried to be or how hard he tried to hide by camouflaging himself. He was green and he had never worked out how to make his skin change.

The only good thing about captivity was that he no longer had to catch his own prey. Food was plentiful and even though he felt ill-fated, he started to grow rapidly.

He vowed that when he escaped, he would exact his revenge on everyone who had made fun of him. Because there were a lot people on his list, he planned to live a long time.

He had two zookeepers. Wedge was rotund. He always wore baggy pants. Clem was tall and skinny. He wore clothes that were too small for him.

As the big snake never moved except to eat, the keepers had become complacent. He had been patient, waiting for them to become careless. They became careless. One day after entering his enclosure they left the door open, and the snake made a mad dash for freedom. Wedge fell over in surprise, but the quick-thinking Clem made a grab at the escapee. As the snake dodged Clem, it accidentally scooted up Wedge's loose pants.

Wedge jerked upright and started screaming and yelling as he ran out of the enclosure. The terrified zookeeper started dancing and twitching in a state of complete panic.

The poor snake got disorientated and instead of leaving the way he had come in, he ended up writhing backwards up the man's thigh as he tried desperately to wriggle free. Unfortunately, just as he managed to get his tail and most of his body free over the man's belt, his protruding fangs got stuck in the elastic at the top of the Wedge's underwear. He was now a big snake.

Helplessly, Clem saw everything. He just kept screaming, "WEDGEY, oh my God, Wedgey …snake… Wedgey… SNAKE!" After his friend fainted, he watched the snake unhook his fangs and slither swiftly away.

Being unclassified, the snake had never had a name… well, never a name that wasn't an insult. Clem had called him a, "Wedgey Snake." It felt right, that was who he was, and he now knew what he had to do to get revenge. He would use his protruding fangs to strike fear into people rather than laughter.

It took the local healer an hour to extract Wedge's jocks from his crack. The people mender had never seen undies stuck as far up someone's bottom before and because the patient's name was Wedge, he named the injury after him. He found it hard to believe that a snake could have possibly caused the injury but he was a professional so he did not scoff out loud where Wedge could hear him.

The Healer treated 10 cases of Wedgiecide over the next week. Every victim blamed a large green snake. A few children who had been to the zoo in the last week were among the victims.

Wedgey snake was feeling pretty proud of himself. He was free and feared and on a roll. One day he came across a Holy man on the top of a hill. The man had been meditating and fasting for forty days and nights. His clothes were loose because of the fasting and the man was sound asleep in a radiant halo of sunlight. Wedgey snake had never had such an easy victim. Using a swift slither which is the snake equivalent of a run up, he gave such a hard wedgie that the man went cross eyed.

Yes Sir, life was good. He was having his idea of fun and Wedgey was now so big that he didn't have to worry about trying to poison or hypnotize his prey, he just gulped it straight down.

Parents started telling their children that they had better behave or the wedgey snake would get them. The wedgey snake revelled in his notoriety. A few children even gave other children wedgies and blamed it on the snake. Kids.

Unfortunately, Wedgey got too big for most breeches and his 'Fangs of Fear' finally became his undoing or rather not undoing them, did him in. His fangs failed to unhook on the biggest pair of underpants he had ever seen. Sadly, the man fainted with fright and the wedgey snake was stuck underneath his enormous backside as he fell backwards.

That is how the wedgey snake became just a green skid mark in the anals of history.

Strangely enough his untimely and slightly disgusting demise may have been a blessing. Even though Wedgey had been unpopular with his fellow serpents when he was younger, his name became cursed for all time by snakes everywhere because the Holy man that he had made cross eyed was none other than St Patrick.

St Patrick's first miracle was to survive the worst wedgie ever given. When St Pat's askance eyesight uncrossed a week later, he was so angry that he banished all snakes from Ireland and while he was at it, he also banished snakes from Greenland, NZ, Iceland and Antarctica though in accordance with banishment attribution laws he is only officially credited with the first banishment.

No matter how hard he tried, he was unable to banish the wedgie from school playgrounds.

What is little known is that St Patrick, after nearly dying of wedgiciditis refused to wear underpants ever again and so as well as being the patron Saint of Ireland he is also the patron Saint of Commandos.

[Historians think that St Pat banished snakes from Greenland because Wedgey was green.The undies that got stuck were white so he also banished snakes from Iceland and Antarctica. It was reported that until he was unwedged, St Patrick spoke in a Kiwi accent, he kept saying, "Ut was a thuck snake, wasn't ut, breu?" so snakes in NZ had no chance. I didn't say they were good historians.]

Authors note: Ok, this is a little bit of a weird one. A long time ago I wrote down one line about a wedgey snake. I thought it was funny and I never forgot about it. I recently dragged that one line from the dark cavern in which it was wisely hiding and here you have it.

Of course it is highly probable that there never were any snakes on the islands of Ireland, NZ, Greenland or Antarctica to be banished but you never know…

16

In a Sandpit Not So Far, Far, Away...

Timmy played for hours, creating a whole city of sand complete with a disguised nuclear waste dump close to a residential area.

He included a huge football stadium decorated with leaves replete with alcohol sponsorship. Timmy is good with detail. He watches the news every night with his parents and that has really helped him with his anxiety attacks.

Sharny and Chancer are 5-year-old peroxide blonde girls. They are sitting on the swings with their brand new 'World's Biggest Teenage Call Girl' dolls. The girls are wearing designer outfits that are disturbingly similar to the few wisps of thread that barely cover certain parts of their dolls. The girls are busy judging the rest of their class through the superficial lens of inappropriate and over sexualized reality TV that they watch but fortunately do not yet understand.

The sandpit is peaceful. Timmy stands up and looks down at his creation – 'Sand City' - it is good buuutt

Timmy knows that the twig forest he had included 'for the environment' has to go. He begins clearing it away to make way for an exclusive gated residential development when a shadow falls across him.

The girls let out an involuntary "ohh, Timmy you're %#@$ed" before they snatch up their busty, scantily clad dolls and race to safety. Timmy is kneeling down; a terrified expression steals onto his face as the shadow looms closer, and closer.

Escape is an attractive option, but it is an option that is unlikely to work. Timmy decides to try anyway but as he tries to get up he is punched and falls heavily on the nuclear waste dump breaking the supposedly 'invincible' sand containing wall and dooming all of the residents of 'Sand City' to painful deaths from radiation poisoning. So much for the safety assurances of the sand box division of the nuclear energy lobby.

More shadows fall on the sand pit. Cronies. A new crony, keen to ingratiate himself sniggers. Unfortunately, he is a premature sniggerer. Good quality cronies are sometimes hard to find.

Basho, the resident kindergarten bully turns and stomps hard on his crony's foot. Timing is everything, laughter at the wrong moment can turn a complete humiliation into a ... a well, an incomplete humiliation.

Basho turns back to his victim, but Timmy has used the distraction to scarper. No one is sniggering now; the sand pit has temporarily become a snigger free zone.

Timmy's face is bruised, and he lies unconvincingly about it to his distracted parents who are actually really happy to believe the totally transparent lie because it means that they don't have to do anything.

Timmy's parents are busy people, too busy to be parents if the truth be known but what do you do when the condom breaks?

Timmy is not quite sure what a condom is, but he does understand that he was an accident so understandably he is reluctant to interrupt the bad news on TV with his own bad news.

17

Wrestling Dad for the Win

Hi, my name is Aelysha. I'm a girl and I like pink and dolls and stuffed animals but I also like to wrestle my Dad and win.

My Dad is over three times as big as me. He says he is only twice as big as me but the bathroom scales don't lie.

I am little but flexible. My Dad is not very stretchy. I've seen him try to touch his toes. It always makes me laugh. When he tries to do it, his fingers are so still so far away from his toes that his toes are lonely. Poor Dad. Poor toes.

When he does push ups I like to help him by climbing on his back. He says this doesn't help at all but if he just concentrated on what he was doing instead of laughing, collapsing or complaining he would get fit a lot faster. Jeepers creepers.

I have an older brother Sam. I've watched Sam wrestle Dad for years and now if Dad starts to win against Sam, I join in. If Dad was ticklish, we could nail him but he is not very ticklish. I think it's because he has a bit of a tum, but I don't tell him that. He says he is just well cushioned. If he did more push ups with me on his back, he would lose that cushion pretty quick. There is just no helping some people.

When Sam is at school, I sometimes wrestle Dad all by myself. Apparently, all the rough play is good for Dads. My little fists and elbows give him a nice massage, and he tends to laugh a lot when we wrestle, even when he is losing, especially when he is losing. Strange. Anyway, I know that laughing is good for him. I notice that adults don't laugh as much as kids, it's like they think they will run out of laughs or something?

Did I say I was strong and clever too? I have noticed a couple of Dad's weaknesses in battle. For example, he likes to nap on weekends, and he can fall asleep really fast or at least he pretends to fall asleep anyway. So when we wrestle, I always make sure that I have plenty of sleep powder with me as I know he is vulnerable to sleep.

If he starts to get the upper hand, I hit him with sleep powder and he has to fall asleep straight away. Sometimes he pretends he didn't hear me, and he keeps going because he thinks that he might finally win. I have to be careful not to hit him with two doses of sleep powder in a row as he will actually try to nap and not get back up, if I let him.

You can learn useful things wrestling. That 'not hearing things' is a pretty good idea and I have started using it myself. I sometimes pretend that I don't hear him when he asks me to pick up my toys.

I use a light tap with my foot to wake him up so we can start the next round. Obviously, my foot is enclosed in an invisible slipper of waking. Using your foot also gives you time to jump back out of reach while he wakes up. Told ya I am clever.

The first time I used it on him, Dad argued that sleep powder wasn't fair. As if me wrestling someone three times as big as me was fair! We were supposed to be wrestling, not arguing! Sheesh. I explained to him that since I was half his size I got to make the rules. I didn't think it was going to help me if I pointed out that I was actually only a third of his size.

If you do this with your Dad just realise that you will have to be a little patient while he gets used to you making all the rules. Start off slow and then once he gets used to sleep powder, hit him with as many new rules as quickly as you can.

The first trick I start with is that Dad can only wrestle me while he is on his knees. Bingo, this immediately cuts down his height advantage.

A couple other tricks I have up my sleeve include: the 'Aelysha Special Paralysing Karate Chop' and the 'No Tickling Spray,' both are pretty self-explanatory and can last a long time - but not too long.

You might let your Dad win a few times. I don't, but it is probably a good idea. Oh, and with the sleep powder just a word of warning, it will be surprising how many times your Dad can 'accidentally' fall asleep and try collapse on your legs. Since he is nearly five times my size it can take me a while to wriggle out of the trap but I am strong and flexible and I can use 'Aelysha's Levitate Dad Wand' if I need to.

Everything I've shared works just as well when I wrestle Mum instead of Dad. A bit of rough play with parents is good for them but just remember that it is about fun not necessarily about winning.

But if you want to win, just follow my guide above.

Authors Note: Aelysha wants me to tell everyone that she did not actually write this, that I wrote it from her perspective. Done.

I loved wrestling, tickling and playing with Sam and Aelysha. A lot of our wrestling started from me giving them horseback rides but when the tired 'horse' got stubborn and stopped, it turned into a wrestle.

With Sam I did have to explain to him that unless we wanted the 'Famous Samuel Knee Drop' to end with Daddy getting a 'Famous drive to hospital to have his ruptured kidney fixed' that he would have to avoid doing the knee drop on certain parts of my body. He also learned very early that punching dad in the balls was a bad idea. I'm guessing that most dads have been hit in the nuts at least once.

Wrestling boys is very physical with lots of pushing and shoving. One of the most important aspects of the play, apart from all the endorphins that get generated from the fun, lies in helping the child to calm down when the game is over. The more practice the child gets in calming down when the game is done, the better they will be when they have to manage their emotions on their own.

As the Dad of a boy, I was well aware of the importance of rough play. What I didn't know and learned, was that my daughter also wanted and needed rough play too, but not too rough and I was also careful to make sure that neither of them ever felt helpless in the game. They were always able to wriggle free.

The rough play with Aelysha was different. It was not as physical as with Sam. Soon after we started to wrestle, she built on some of Sam's ideas and invented some original rules of her own with perhaps some assistance from watching Pokemon.

18

T'was Christmas Day
(A modern sequel to 'T'was the Night Before Christmas)

T'was Christmas Day and all through the house
All the creatures were stirring, even the mouse
Tummies full of tasty treats big and small
Toys and wrapping paper strewn through the hall
A bicycle half ridden was parked 'neath the tree
Next to a teddy, stocking, train and golf tee

There was rumbling and tumbling and shrieks of laughter
With all of the activity, it was a wonder the plaster
Didn't fall from the ceiling to join in the fun
Yawns replaced giggles as the day was near done
Into new jammies, teeth brushed into bed
One story that's all, big hug, kiss on the head

The house was a mess, a holy mess at that
In the middle of the signs of joy I sat
With a smile and a sigh I remembered the day
As my beautiful spouse on my lap she did lay
Our little man Sam's first Christmas aware
Of anticipation, of thrills, his presents, his share

An early start to be sure, "Is it Christmas today, Dad?"
I ventured forth to see if Santa'd been, he had.
The door was opened and running full pelt
Sam raced to the tree where with a heart felt
Tremble of excitement, of delight, of glee
"Mum, Dad are these presents for me?"

We sat next the tree and the presents did share
From Grandma and Grandpa, Uncle Chris, Auntie Clair
The presents, well wrapped, with love they did come
Were opened, checked out and of course there were some
That were just the perfect gifts for a boy nearly four
Who opened our presents too and still asked for more

There is something about a child's unbridled joy
So I watched in wonder as Sam opened each toy
And I thanked my God for this special event
Which goes on each day to a lesser extent
To live in the now, to take joy from each minute
We need to re-learn this, us adults, this planet

As we sit and give thanks, we hear a small bump
What would have caused this unexpected thump?
From near the tree it came, so to there we do haste
A blanket and Sam, toy in hand, smile on face
Fast asleep, near his presents, the tree burning bright
A special moment, a surprise. We tuck him in and say "goodnight."

Authors note: This poem was indeed inspired by Sam's first Christmas aware and he did fall asleep near the tree with a toy in his hand and a smile on his face. I researched 'A Visit from St. Nicholas' and have included stories I wrote based on that poem

The Night Before Christmas – Or Was It?

'A Visit From St. Nicholas,' also known as 'The Night Before Christmas' was first published anonymously in December, 1823 in the Troy (New York) Sentinel. It is considered the most famous Christmas poem ever written and it is the foundation on which the modern persona of Santa Claus is irrevocably based.

Interestingly the poem was never copyrighted, which contributed significantly to its popularity. It was not until 1844 that the authorship of the poem was claimed. Stranger still is the current controversy about who really did pen the famous poem that put the patron saint of children in a sleigh pulled by eight tiny reindeer.

Legend has it that Clement Clark Moore (1779-1863) wrote the immortal poem on Christmas Eve, 1822 after a sleigh ride home from Greenwich Village.

He had dashed out to buy a turkey to be included in a basket of goodies for distribution to the poor of the neighborhood.

Inspired by the moonlight on the snow, the holiday season and the bright starlit sky he was moved to write a few lines appropriate to St. Nicholas. Apparently Moore was so inspired that he composed the entire 56 line poem in his head and then wrote it down perfectly. Yeah, right.

Moore read the poem to his family on that very Christmas Eve, stressing that it was only for them. A family friend learnt of the poem from the children and sometime later copied it. She submitted it to the Troy Sentinel on the condition that the author was to remain anonymous.

Soon, the poem was published in other newspapers, almanacs and magazines until it became the most published Christmas poem of all time. In 1844, the modest Moore first claimed authorship of the famous verses by including 'A Visit from St. Nicholas' in a small book of his poetry, imaginatively entitled 'Poems,' which he published at the request of his children.

What a perfectly, lovely, cheery Christmas story. But is it true? Does it not seem odd that Moore waited so long to claim authorship? Before publishing 'Poems,' Moore wrote to the proprietor of the Troy Sentinel, Norm Tuttle. The letter from Tuttle to Moore is held in the Museum of the City of New York. In this letter, Tuttle wrote "…at the time of its publication I did not know who the author was – but have since been informed that you were the author." Only after receiving this 'all clear' response did Clement Clark Moore put his name to the verses by publishing it in 'Poems.'

There is however another claimant to the authorship of 'A Visit From St. Nicholas.' The descendants of Major Henry Livingston, Jr. (1748-1828) believe that Henry penned the great poem and read it to his children as early as 1807.

It seems that sometime before 1822, a governess visited the Livingstons. She was so taken with a certain poem that she asked Henry for a copy of it and he obliged. This Governess went to work for a family 'down south' and on the way she stopped in NYC and left a copy of the poem with, drum roll please, Clement Moore.

Henry Livingston died in 1828, never knowing of Moore's appropriation of his poem. Henry's son Sidney later found the original manuscript of the poem with corrections and cross outs but it was unfortunately destroyed in a house fire.

It was not until 1860 that Sidney's family actually came across a copy of the poem with Moore's name on it. Whilst incensed, the family decided not to publicly proclaim Henry's authorship against Moore's because Moore was high in the Episcopalian Church and many of Henry's family were ministers or married to ministers in the Episcopalian Church.

The first descendant to successfully bring the conflicting authorship claims to the public's attention was William Sturges Thomas, in 1920. After publication in major New York City newspapers there was quite a buzz, but the stories faded and Moore's claim seemed as solid as ever.

The major breakthrough for the deceased major came in the year 2000, when Don Foster, literary forensic detective and English Professor at Vassar College, New York, was convinced by Mary Van Deusen to investigate authorship of 'A Visit From St. Nicholas.'

After extensive analysis Foster concluded that Clement C. Moore could not have been the author of the poem and that it was probably the work of Livingston. Foster's analysis of this literary deception appears in his book, *Author Unknown: On the Trail of Anonymous* (New York: Henry Holt, 2000). Mary Van Deusen later heard the story that the names of the reindeer were the names of the horses in Henry's stable though she has not been able to verify this. The authorship of the poem remains contentious.

By all descriptions Clement C. Moore was quite a serious, scholarly chap and one can speculate that his six children were simply overjoyed when he read them the fun and frivolous tale of St. Nick.

When asked by his delighted children if he wrote the poem, it is possible that a slightly embarrassed Moore confided to them in a moment of weakness that indeed he had but that they must keep the poem a secret. Never did he expect that a small fib could be so magnificently exposed.

Imagine Moore's discomfort when, against his wishes, a copy of the poem escapes his home and makes its way into Christmas history. Moore will not have been the first parent to lie to his children nor will he have been the last but with Santa apparently checking his naughty and nice list twice, as parents, we'd better be careful what we say to our children because there is no guarantee that it will stay in-house.

Blixem Doomed From the Word On!

St. Nick changes reindeer line up! Few people realize that the eight names that we know so well, were not the original stable of St. Nicholas's famous reindeer. The first eight for St. Nick in 1823 were;

Now! Dasher, now! Dancer, now! Prancer, and Vixen, On! Comet, on! Cupid, on! Dunder and Blixem;

Blixem? Poor Blixem. Blixem became the first recorded reindeer scratching. Blixem had hardly got out of his harness from his 1824 Christmas tour of duty when he was replaced by the now familiar Blitzen. Spokes-deer Vixen confirmed that there was both rhyme and reason for the change and that Blixem just didn't fit in with the rest of the troupe. This did leave some of the other flying reindeer a little uneasy, none more so than little Dunder.

The awkward rhythm of the original 'urging on' by St. Nick was further modified by Norman Tuttle in 1830 following an unfortunate mid-air incident where Dunder and Blitzen failed to dash away quickly enough and the ensuing tangle of antlers, harness and sled nearly sent St. Nick spiraling into a snow covered field. Dunder quietly left St. Nick's coursers to be replaced by the racier Donder in about 1837. He was not available for comment.

St. Nick's starting line thus became the names we are so familiar with:

"Now, Dasher! now, Dancer! now, Prancer and Vixen! On, Comet! on, Cupid! on, Donder and Blitzen!"

Some yuletide historians believe that whilst St. Nicholas was reluctant to tamper with his team after the early axing of Blixem, he just never fully regained his confidence in Dunder which left the North Pole barn door wide open for the ambitious and charismatic Donder to eventually edge him out.

Santa stayed with his tried and tested team for nearly one hundred years until 'one foggy Christmas Eve' in 1936. But the story of the ninth reindeer is one for another time. What goes on in the flying reindeer stable, stays in the flying reindeer stable but suffice it to say that it took quite some time before all the reindeer loved little Rudolph.

19

Parent Teacher Teacher Child

In the Western world not so very long ago the prevailing parenting paradigm was that children were to be seen but not heard and ideally not seen too often.

Under this type of highly authoritarian parenting pattern the knowledge transference premise was that of a strictly policed and sometimes cruelly enforced one way street. All data flowed from the omnipotent parents to the child supplicant. Such a system is destined for failure though the magnitude of the failing takes years or even decades to become obvious. Is it obvious enough now?

Parenting is not a one way street. For me it isn't even a two way street. It is more like a clover leaf with community, family and intergenerational interests creating complex information flows with frequent bumps and scrapes and the occasional quite messy pileup.

My first born, Samuel, started teaching me in utero. He helped me to grow up. Sam was not a planned pregnancy. I was not asked if I was ready to become a father and had I been asked my emphatic answer would have been, "No way! Just look at me." My fair assumption being that one glance at my selfish, self-centered, sometimes childish ways would have been worth at least a thousand words.

If Sam had waited until I was ready to become a dad then he could still be waiting. I am eternally grateful that he did not wait.

I was really scared of becoming a father, of becoming responsible for another human being. The prospect of becoming a Dad freaked me out. My life was going to change big time and I knew that to be a good Dad I would have to let go of some of my boyish ways that no longer served me but that were comfortable and familiar.

I admit that there was a part of me that just wanted to solve my dilemma by running away. Fortunately before Sam was born I somehow got my head around fatherhood and I embraced it. I started to get excited about becoming a Dad. Sure, I was still terrified and there have been challenging, frustrating times but they have been vastly outweighed by the many times when being a parent is a privilege, an amazing and rewarding journey beyond words.

I have found my children to be astonishingly gifted and dedicated teachers and learners too. You could have told me how clever and amazing children are but until I had my own, I would have never fully comprehended the truth of what you were saying.

Their gifts to me have mostly been emotional lessons. Until recently I was rarely given gifts of knowledge (besides how to operate the remote control) but now that they are older and natives to a web connected, technology driven world that has changed too, especially teaching me how to use my phone.

Most importantly, Samuel and Aelysha have opened my heart in ways I did not know it could open. Just as children arrive without an instruction book so too my heart has no manual.

I was 33 when I first held my son in my arms. My heart's blood pumping rate was still prime / sub-prime but my heart's love rate was constricted. My heart had a lot of scar tissue from old emotional hurts and wounds both real and imagined. As with all muscles, we either use it or lose it.

My children (and spouse too) have helped my heart muscle to stay supple. Hardening of hearts moves the world away from compassion and towards a massive global coronary. Interestingly, heart disease and cardio vascular diseases are the number one killers of people according to the World Health Organisation.

My children remind me that happiness does not have to be earned, that love is unconditional and that joy can be taken from the simplest of pleasures. They remind me of what it is to feel wonder and awe. As Samuel and Aelysha have grown, I have grown too. It is amazing when I contemplate that the baby I could hold in one hand, now towers over me as a young man.

At times my children have mirrored aspects of me that I have not always been comfortable seeing. I have said, "I don't know where they get that from?" BUT even as I said it, I knew. I knew where they got it BUT no one had told me that children can pick up on the stuff I say to myself even if I have never said it out loud.

Children are fluent in subliminal. It is weird to hear a familiar inner dialogue being repeated when I would rather it was not and they also obviously pick up stuff from their non-parental environment too.

One day, I was driving and listening to ABC radio when I heard an economist and parent espousing how much economic sense it makes to have children in child care centers from an early age; how it frees both parents to work which adds to a nation's productivity and GDP. He argued that the statistics from the studies that he chose to read argued that children were not adversely affected by outsourcing parental responsibilities to for-profit child care centers though he did not phrase it that way.

This economist was a one way street kind of guy. Apparently, it is fine for children to take an emotional bullet for the sake of the economy. The God of economic rationalism says that efficiency is everything and should be applied to raising children and also managing the elderly. But all offerings to this insatiable deity measure and promote only that which sits comfortably on the altar. Overwhelming evidence that worshipping economic rationalism is leading us rapidly to our extinction is derided and ignored.

It is really very simple. Our children cannot teach us if we are not present for their lessons and they need us to be there for them when they need us, not when it is convenient for them to need us. Too many parents are truant, wagging their parental responsibility. Lessons of the bliss that comes from unconditional love, of joy, of patience, more patience, of compassion, of patience, of laughter; of patience each of these lessons is specially designed for us.

Children also have an uncanny way of presenting us with opportunities to deal with emotional issues from our own childhood that need completion. Child care workers cannot work through our 'stuff' for us. If we miss the lessons through absenteeism there are no podcasts to watch or notes to copy and words struggle to capture the experience of moments of connection; sharing a blissed out smile, spontaneous laughter and creativity and of basking in unconditional love. Tiny fingers curling around my finger doesn't sound like much and it can be incredibly moving.

Children are not 'valuable human capital' - they are valuable, precious, small human beings. Our culture does not treat our children as precious beyond lip service or parenting as important. We live in a society where the lights are on but where too often no one is home for the children and where there is little community support for struggling parents and all the 'lost' boys and girls.

Stress and depression are already at epidemic levels and shockingly but not surprisingly they are now even infecting young children. The World Health Organisation predicts that depression will be the leading cause of disease burden worldwide by 2030[1].

Parenting can be challenging enough when feeling perky and connected. Adding emotional and or financial stress to the parenting mix is a recipe for disaster especially for single parents who do not have someone that can tag them out when they have not only lost the plot but lost the entire book as well.

Despite dire health and well-being forecasts it seems that more money is being channeled into how to exploit declining mental health rather than creating the fundamental societal changes that are required to remedy it.

The economist went on to say that being in childcare didn't seem to affect his children. How would he know? How many practice children has he raised to adulthood to be able to judge that? Miss those early years and the bonding that helps us when things get tough is weak or absent and there will definitely be some tough days.

In thoroughbred horses the bonding between mare and foal is protected, fostered and sacrosanct - every child is a thoroughbred.

You can get any answer you want if you ask the right questions. Methinks some of the questions *el economisto* asks his children may be a little leading "You're OK with Mummy and Daddy working all the time aren't you?"

The proper answer for a very eloquent one year old is: "No, I'm not OK with you working all the time. You and my mother are the most important people in the world to me and I never see you, you never sit on the floor and play with me. You are constantly stressed which makes me stressed. I love you unconditionally now but you are supposed to my parents and you'll find out in about twelve or fifteen years how not OK I am but thanks for taking the time to ask a token question you selfish asshole! I am sorry that being a good parent is such a hollow ungratifying experience for you."

I am not saying no childcare at all. I am saying there needs to be a balance and the thought of babies that should still be on the breast being left for long days at day care centers makes me sad.

Children are not SIMS and there is no Undo button but there is guilt and regret later. A child cannot conveniently put their little life on stasis until the parents have career, house and financial shit all together.

I got quite cranky listening to this smug jerk and I started shouting at the radio even though it was only talk back. It probably didn't help that the man being interviewed was an economist, one of the high priests of economic rationalism.

It is often quoted that it takes a village to raise a child. It takes a community to raise the child and also to support the parents and to take care of the grandparents. Strong communities are vital for our emotional well-being. I would love to see more money being devoted to community services, big well-resourced centers, halls, parks and libraries, big bright cheerful libraries that everyone can use.

One of the phrases that people loved to say to me when Sam was a newborn was, "They grow up so quick." As a brand new parent I kind of went, "whatever," but by the time Sam was one, I was already saying it to parents of younger babies because, 'They do grow up so very quickly' and our time with them is fleeting.

I am a long way off becoming a grandfather – then this story will be: 'Grandparent and parent the teachers to the child, and child and grandchild teacher to the parents and grandparents.' Not a great title for a sequel but then I have time to work on it.

1 http://apps.who.int/gb/ebwha/pdf_files/EB130/B130_9-en.pdf

20

Where has my Pedestal Gone?

Feet of clay. All parents have feet of clay. It is not bad. It is not actually a design flaw. It comes with the job and it is healthy and painful at the same time. Knowing that you have feet of clay can lessen the hurt and it makes it possible to avoid the following monologue:

"Wait a second. How did I get clay there?"

"Those rotten kids throwing mud at me. I'll just brush it off… Huh? It's not rubbing off but my foot is… crumbling? BOTH of my feet are crumbling?"

"What the…?"

"Now I'm falling off my pedestal. WELL, THAT'S JUST GREAT!"

<Whiney voice> "Awww, this isn't fair! I liked the view from up there. I liked the children looking up to me. <sniff> I was up there for over a decade."

"I DON'T WANNA FALL DOWN!"

<CUE tantrum><END SCENE>

<CUE possibility of second tantrum>

It is awkward and it happens.

I remember watching TV footage of the toppling of a life size statue of Stalin – ropes were used to pull the despot's cenotaph off his perch. Stalin's statue did not have clay feet because no sculptor would ever make such a figurine – especially not one for a murderous dictator. Designing a statue that has clay feet would be considered insane because clay and metal do not bond well and the statue would be inherently weak and would inevitably collapse. The only unknown for a statue with feet of clay is how long it will take for the feet to turn to powder.

The awesome thing about being a parent is that our children will put us up on a pedestal, even if we don't always deserve it. The size of the pedestal, how solid the base is and how long we stay up there is unknown. Eventually we have to vacate that place for the child to grow up. A parent's job is to ensure that we have terra cotta feet. The good news is, the statues of their peers, the ones that will replace us, also have clay feet.

To a baby it must seem like their parents have superhuman powers. We are 4 or 5 times their height and 20 to 30 times their mass and strong? We can lift them effortlessly and also throw them high into the air and catch them safely. I could hold my babies in one hand. I was faster than a crawling infant, more powerful than something really powerful and I could leap tall Lego structures with a single bound. Pretty amazing, huh? My only kryptonite was, and still is, those evil green miniature cabbages called *Brussel sprouts, yuuuuuuuuuuuuuuuuuuck. But I digress.

The degrees of difficulty to perform superhuman feats of strength increase as the baby gets bigger. Holding onto Sam's wrists and spinning him around and around in a circle was really easy… for a while. No matter how many times we did it, there was always a request for, "Please, just one more." I also held him by the ankles and spun him around like that and I was frequently asked to do the advanced child spin combo of holding onto one leg and one wrist. The best time to stop spinning is just before the hernia.

The 'Magic carpet' on the beach trick quickly became a drag, literally. It was not a complicated stunt and on a joy for effort basis it is heavy on the parental effort BUT with a high joy output. It is devastatingly simple. The child's job is to sit on one end of a large beach towel, that is it. The job of the 'Hero' with the superpowers is to hold the opposite end and use it to pull the child along the sand as if they were sitting on a magic carpet. The accompanying giggles and laughter do make the load lighter but the constant commands to "go faster, faster," dampen that effect. Tight turns can temporarily relieve the parent of the payload but may result in accusations of, "You did that on purpose!" which are difficult to refute.

The child may choose to face the source of propulsion, but watching the pathetic, puffing, panting and at times complaining parent is less attractive than leaning backwards into the towel and gazing out to the horizon. The duration of the ride depends on the fitness and sheer determination of the person towing and the nagging prowess of the towee. Good times. Some short rides, some longer, all fun.

As a parent we don't have comic book style super powers but for a while, at least, our children think of us as Heroes and we do have huge positional power. Our positional power is bestowed upon us, not by study or by having earned it, but by donating DNA. The biological act of a sperm fertilising an egg bestowed upon me the job title of, 'Parent.' Beth did a bit more than that to earn her title. Okay, a lot more than that but effectively we became the bosses o fa helpless newborn baby at birth.

Imagine that you are being interviewed for what has been described as the most important job in the world:

INTERVIEWER: "So, Mr. Jones, thank you for applying for this job. As you know this is a very, very important position with a lot of responsibility. You will basically become responsible for another human being. Let's just check your qualifications... so, ummm, do you have a penis?"

MR. JONES: "Yes, sir. I call him the <insert the name of your penis here>."

INTERVIEWER: <shakes head> <sarcasm> "Excellent."

INTERVIEWER (CONT'D): "Last thing on the list, Mr. Jones. It is a surprisingly short list for such an important job, are your sperm motile?"

MR. JONES: "Oh, yeah, real motile. Very... What's motile?"

INTERVIEWER: "Can they swim?"

MR. JONES: "Oh, yeah, champions."

INTERVIEWER: "Well, that does it. Congratulations, you are fully qualified."

MR. JONES: "But don't I need any training? Don't I have to read any books? Learn poop disposal techniques? Leadership training?"

INTERVIEWER: "Nope – you have the whole package - penis and sperm – for you, that's it."

The biology of becoming a parent is well understood. In fact, parenting is the only job I have ever applied for where I didn't even know that I was applying for the job, when I was on the job.

Our role in raising a child is an amazing journey that will inevitably bring us into conflict with them. Getting them to do what they want to do is easy, peasy, but when we want the young 'un to do something that they do not want to do: things as Dickensian as picking up their clothes or doing the dishes or stop hitting their sister, there will be 'situations.' Our statue will likely wobble back and forth a little from the tremors of these events but the clay stays surprisingly resilient for many years.

There will inevitably come a time when our child will try to sack us. They will dispute our authority, our right to govern, by declaring to us that; "You're not the boss of me!" but until they reach legal age, we are.

No one likes to be bullied. It is not acceptable in the playground or in the workplace. A lot of bosses abuse their corporation granted positional power. Finally, more and more people are standing up and saying that bullying is not OK in the workplace but even the best personnel policy edicts and Interpersonal Skills Courses find it hard to overcome behavioural patterns that have often been in place since a person's childhood. The old command and control style of management which 'dominated' business culture and also parenting for so long is outdated and should be consigned to the fossil record.

Bullying in the home is also not acceptable. As Uncle Ben says over and over and over again in 'Spiderman,' "With great power, comes great responsibility." So it is with parents. We have great power over our children. We have to learn how to use this power wisely. We live in a world where the presiding parenting paradigm, Authoritarian Parenting, has been based on controlling and dominating the child. Fortunately, this way of parenting is fading. In my opinion, the authoritarian parenting style is predicated on the abuse of positional power. It is not based on respect for the small human being in our care. Total abdication of our positional power, which happens in Permissive Parenting, is also highly ineffective.

Authoritative parenting is based on connection and it takes a larger investment of parental time which is time well spent. The authoritarian parent produces short term behavioural modifications in their children based on <shudder> shaming, smacking and/or threatening but this is actually bullying behaviour that is not tolerated in any progressive company so why should we allow it in our homes? Hitting children has now been banned in 49 countries. If your 80-year-old aunty refused to eat her Brussel sprouts, would you hit her? And remember those clay feet I was talking about?

The weakness in the feet of the statue of the parent is activated when the growing child realises for the first time that their parent is a mortal human being and is fallible and makes mistakes like every other human being on the planet. The child-like awe for the amazing array of parental superpowers wanes. They will likely ask you to stop wearing your "Super Parent" cape. The cracks in your heel and between your toes will get wider and wider.

Instead of cries for, "One more time," our actions, if they are dignified with speech at all, may elicit, "Really?" Or "Whatever." 'Eye Yoga,' where the teenager practices rolling their eyes becomes popular. The timing and grace of the parental pedestal dismount is unique for each family. For some it is precipitous, some calamitous, some gradual and some parents claim that they were pushed. Some parents refuse to 'stand down' even after the pedestal has been well and truly blown up.

Highly authoritarian parents in particular will pour concrete over their earthen feet and try to stay on the pedestal for as long as possible, refusing the inevitable. It never ends well, for no matter how many coats of manipulation or threats are applied, there will always be an exposed Achilles heel or Achilles toenail or Achilles tendon or all three.

It will happen. One day, you will realise that in public your child is walking a few paces ahead of you instead of beside you. The hugs that once were so welcome by your child are now not well welcomed. Reminding them that they used to love "Eensie-weensie spider" and "This little piggy went to market" or the colour pink is not appreciated or funny even if delivered with great aplomb. It is different and part of the healthy progression of the relationship between parent and child. It is part of the cycle of the child growing into a young adult. To do this, they push away from us and they put their peers on the pedestal that we used to occupy. This can be pretty difficult to adapt to, especially if our former pride of place is taken up by people that we don't like.

As a parent we remember when our young adult was a totally helpless infant who relied on us for everything. For most of their life span they have been little children to us, so adjusting to a new relationship with a towering teenager can be tricksy.

There are things that we can do to assist this important transition, to help us clean our calves of the dried red mud. To adjust to and honour the transformation from child to young adult. A contemporary, community based Rite of Passage can be very helpful for the entire family. I was privileged to work for a harm prevention charity, The Pathways Foundation that rans 'Pathways to Manhood' and 'Pathways into Womanhood' programs. Honouring and assisting people through our various life stage transitions makes a lot of sense. We've tried doing nothing for thousands of years and look at how well that is working out for us. Life stages are important: Child to young adult, young adult to adult, adult to parent, older to elder and then the ultimate transition, death.

So, my name is Daniel, and I had a dream. In that dream I saw a bronze statue that had feet of clay. I looked up and the face of the statue was mine and it was smiling and a tear was also running down one cheek. When the tear touched the clay, the clay softened to mud and the statue fell off its pedestal and lay on its side.

The heart of the statue never stopped beating. The statue took some time to come to terms with its new perspective. The heart kept beating. With patience and effort, the statue grew new feet. Slowly, awkwardly, the statue stood up and shook off its thin outer coating of bronze revealing the flesh and blood mortal underneath. A smaller human appeared next to the statue and together, they strode forward.

<u>* Authors Note on Brussel Sprouts</u>. I hate Brussel sprouts. I don't say this to offend any sproutists but when I was little we were always told we had to eat all the food on our plates before we could leave the table. I heartily endorsed this policy when it came to pizza, lasagne, Spanish rice and desert but, yeah, you guessed it, it created a lot of conflict when I was confronted with a serving of those… those, things.

I tried everything to avoid eating them, but they were too big to hide under the edge of the plate and our dog refused to help me. Bad dog! Smart dog. I sometimes had to stay at the table a long time after everyone else had left. I forfeited deserts too. To get them off my plate I would put some in my mouth and holding back a strong gag reflex I would dash to the toilet and spit them out as quickly as I could and hope I didn't follow through with a spew. Yes, my reaction was that strong.

Imagine my delight when I stumbled across this article published in the UK Telegraph Newspaper: <u>Scientists discover that Neanderthals hated Brussel sprouts</u>. Oh, joy! I have been called a Neanderthal before but I had always taken it as an insult rather than a compliment. It seems that my sproutly vomit reflex is at least partly genetic. Brussel sprouts are cabinoids and they contain compounds very similar to phenylthiocarbamide (PTC). Some poisonous plants have PTC in them. The loathing of any bitter taste that smacks of PTC in an evolutionary context makes sense. My body is trying to protect me from eating something which might be poisonous. Much better to not eat poison than to eat poison. D'uh. For a lot of people, the gene that controls this response is recessive.

As a child, obviously I didn't have a doctorate in Biochemistry that would have enabled me to explain research that had not even been started to my parents. I wasn't trying to be naughty or rebellious or disobedient by not eating Brusselsprouts – they made me physically ill. It was a long time ago – maybe my reaction has changed but being forced to eat them has made it personal between me and my kryptonite. I have told my children to refer to Brussel sprouts as 'evil little green balls of vomit.' BUT they don't do that. Actually, they kind of like eating them. In fact, they will ask Beth to cook them. I think it is just so they can watch me squirm. The scamps.

Sure there was also some food that I just didn't like but maybe, just maybe there is a reason why your child refuses to eat a certain food. Just saying, authoritative parenting can reduce a lot of unnecessary conflict.

If you are looking for a book that can help you understand the differences between Authoritarian and Authoritative parenting and how to set boundaries and maintain maximum connection with your children, I highly recommend Robin Grille's book "Heart to Heart Parenting."

21

The Parent Olympics

The 2008 Beijing Olympics were followed by the Paralympics, as usual, but then there was a more unusual and less publicised event that was organised for the 900 million hard working peasants in China, the Peasant Olympics, also called the National Peasant Games.

The peasant games include; the '60-metre Plastic Rice Seedling Transplanting Race,' the '60-metre Snatch the Grain and get it into Storage Race' where contestants load a 'harvest' of sandbags onto three-wheeled bikes and sprint for the tape, the 'Water Carrying Contest' to protect the seedlings amid drought and more common sports too. I am not making this up; it is a quadrennial event that started in 1988.

In Nimbin, NSW there is the annual Marijuana Olympics as part of the Mardi Grass celebration. Events include; the 'Iron Growers Event' where athletes lug a sack of fertiliser and a bucket of water through an obstacle course which includes a tick and leech infested tunnel; the 'Bong Throw and Yell' event; the 'Guess the Correct Weight" event and various 'Joint Rolling' events. Also, not making this up.

These non-IOC sanctioned Olympics got me thinking about an Olympics that would honor the largest group of people on the planet, parents.

The Parent Olympics or Parentlympics would have some very special contests. The 'Catch, Drop, Clean, and Release' would have a distinct rodeo feel to it. Over tired and hungry two and a half year olds with bursting dirty nappies would be released into a corral where a parent would have to catch the toddler, remove the dirty nappy, clean the dirty butt, put a fresh nappy on and then release the child without getting covered in poo or sprayed with wee. The quickest time wins. No ropes or other restraints are allowed and points are deducted for leaving any poop on the kid. Any parent who swears at or threatens a child is instantly disqualified.

Other events would include the Parentathlon also known as the 'Morning School Bus Challenge.' Children are woken by the starting gun and parents have to navigate the following gates; find the socks, dress them, make breakfast, make school lunches and deliver them to the bus stop location before the bus leaves. Mismatched socks are fine but both a right and left shoe must be worn to access the bus.

Points are deducted for children leaving homework behind and for giving the right lunch box to the wrong kid. Bonus points are available for preparing nutritious breakfasts and lunches. In the finals, the children will produce a note at the last moment that has to be signed before they can get on the bus.

The 'Teenage Hurdles' is the most challenging event I can think of. It would be sheep dog trial'ish. Two teenage boys would be in a pen / room playing an Xbox or PlayStation (depends on sponsorship) and two teenage girls would be on social media via their 'smart' phones. The parent has to herd the teens out of the pen and into a kitchen where a stack of dirty dishes has been left. This event is the parental equivalent of the 4 minute mile before Roger Bannister – it has never been done.

The 'Find the Toddler Race' promises drama filled heats. A parent would be placed in a crowd with his or her toddler. The parent would receive a phone call from a race official which the parent must answer to start the clock. Of course, during this momentary distraction, the child will disappear into the crowd and the parent then has to find their child as quickly as possible. The crowd will maintain steady indifference to the parent's quest. Nearly every parent has had a go at 'Find the Toddler' but some parent children combinations have had more practice than others.

My favourite event though would be the '100m Non-Dash Whilst Holding the Hand of an Eighteen Month Old.' The world record for this event is 55 minutes and it is not held by a Kenyan. Bribing or dragging the child to hurry them along is not permissible. Breaking hand contact is instant disqualification.

I remember very fondly, holding Sam's little hand and walking along Commercial Road in Melbourne. I was in no hurry and he was so little. I was and still am such a proud Dad.

We covered every bit of 100m in 55 minutes to take the world record. In this event, it is the quality of the journey not the speed that counts. The wonder and joy of almost every step was extraordinary.

I shuffled along at Sam's pace. We got lapped by a snail. We were slow, partly because of his small legs and partly because there was so much to see and do. We stopped often

– sometimes we stopped for Sam to pick up a 'treasure' from the ground. The rocks and bottle tops were ok, but I encouraged him to drop the 'yukky' cigarette butts as quickly as possible. We paused for every tram that trundled past. Each one elicited an excited "TRAM! TRAM!" as he tested his rapidly growing vocabulary. Not every truck got an exclamation but most buses did and 'lello' cars. We also saw a 'PLANE, PLANE.'

Everything was exciting and wondrous. Sam's bright blue eyes were constantly looking up and down, left and right.

I was aware that I had developed tunnel vision. I had stopped looking around, stopped appreciating my environment. I was constantly looking only towards my destination. It is a common adult affliction. I try to remember to look at the world as if I am a child and I fail miserably at this.

Sam was just drinking in his environment as we went along. I loved his curiosity, his natural delight and his confidence. He was exploring and I was his guide and protector.

I will always treasure the memory of the absolute trust and unconditional love that was transmitted to me by the touch of those tiny fingers.

Whilst the thought of a Parent Olympics tickles my inner comic, parenting is not supposed to be competitive because it is not a sporting event, it is a lifelong commitment.

A 100m running track stays a 100m running track from the time it is created until the time it is destroyed, the path and rules do not vary. An athlete knows precisely where he or she starts the race and where he or she finishes and every step in the dead straight line in between.

Parenting starts differently for every parent and there is simply no finish line. The track is anything but straight and every child and every parent is unique and constantly changing.

I have met some parents who are highly competitive and they annoy the crap out of me. Competitiveness begets competitiveness and at times I have risen to the bait of competivity and I may have even baited the odd hook along the way. I don't like it when I do it. It is usually the result of my own insecurity.

Every parent that loves their child and strives to be a good parent deserves a place on a podium and even as we step up and have the ribbon placed around our necks we know, that as our children grow, we will fall off our podium and that that is ok.

We don't need a Parentlympic but there are a few events that are worth running every day: How can I be the best parent possible? And what am I grateful for? Striving for a personal best in these events is not about competition, it is about great parenting.

Authors note: Did anyone notice how similar the 'Iron Grower' event sounded to the '60-metre snatch the grain and get it into storage race?' Wonder if any senior Chinese officials have ever been to Nimbin on a 'cultural' exchange?

If you still think I am making any of this up look up MardiGrass and here is a link to the National Peasant Games: https://en.wikipedia.org/wiki/National_Peasants%27_Games

22

Dancing with Whales

It was a beautiful calm, sunny day and we were at one of our local beaches in northern NSW with a friend and his two little boys.

For weeks, the seas had been rough and the ocean brown and dirty looking due to all the storms we'd been having. We were all delighted to have a day at the beach and the water was amazing; crystal clear and clean and blue and brisk and invigorating and my words still fall miserably short of describing just how fantastic it was.

Samuel and his six year old friends were swimming like little seals in the surf near the shore. They'd swim and splash around until they were blue and shivering then they would race out and roll in the warm fine dry sand at the top of the beach just long enough for their teeth to stop chattering before they charged back into the surf to rinse and repeat the process.

Aelysha, our toddler, delighted in holding our hands so she could walk in the shallow water until she was purple. We would then lift her out of the water to an impressive medley of kicks and screams, dry her off and warm her up only to spot her crawling back to the water grinning wildly as soon as our backs were turned. ... "Aelysha ... Aelysha" the surf sirens would call "they are looking the other way... come to us". That's her story anyway.

I was walking back up the beach on the way to the car (again) on some child related imperative (it was in fact a dash for Aelysha's hat, the one she gleefully throws off and runs away from) when I looked up the beach and saw humpback whales surfacing just outside the breakers.

We had been glimpsing whales from the beach at New Brighton for the past couple of weeks but they hadn't been nearly as close to shore as this.

All we had seen of the annual migration so far had been the odd wave of their flukes or the spume blasts from their blowholes. We had been excited each time we saw them. It is excellent to see a whale anytime but this time, well, this was more, this was an opportunity.

I dashed back to our sandy 'base camp,' snatched the face mask from my bag and raced down the beach, yelling as I went to everyone else to watch the whales coming up the beach before I dove into the surf and started swimming.

I'd always wanted to swim with whales and dolphins. I have done a lot of snorkeling and scuba diving over many years but had never experienced it. This was my chance and I went for it. Unfortunately, I was as unfit as I'd ever been and the edge of the breakers proved to be quite a bit further away than they had looked from the beach.

By the time I finally got out behind the breakers I was puffing pretty hard. I immediately looked towards where I hoped the whales would be but there was nothing there. They had already swum past me. I had missed them.

I was already berating myself for being too slow when I turned in the opposite direction and I saw this huge humpback heading straight for me. She had swum past me but had turned around.

She was graceful, beautiful and very, very large. It sounds like the bleeding obvious and I shouldn't have been surprised but I was.

It suddenly occurred to me that all I was wearing was a face mask. I experienced a touch of nerves and a slight tightening of my sphincter. My goal was coming straight for me and I was suddenly a bit nervous, getting hit with a big barnacled flipper or tail was *not* on my bucket list.

Before I knew it she dove right under me and I could clearly see her and I also saw a light grey calf tucked in close to her body. They were very gentle and serene.

I'm sure they knew I was there and I was so close I think I could have touched them with my foot but I crouched up anyway. They glided under me and as quickly as they had appeared they were gone and I was alone with the adrenalin and the excitement of the moment.

It was an amazing experience to swim with wild whales, one I will never forget. Why any nation or person would ever want to kill one of these magnificent beings is beyond my comprehension.

My experience with the whales also gave me an interesting life analogy. How many of us have goals which we are quite happy with being goals forever? You know, things or events or outcomes that we want but deep down we're not quite sure if we really deserve them but it doesn't really matter anyhow because they are only goals and they seem as far away as the moon, especially when we've held these goals for a long time.

If we give up on our goals or hopes then the chances of ever attaining them decline precipitously. A little preparation can go a long way. I hadn't given up on my goal of swimming with whales and I had packed and carried my face mask dozens of times without ever using it.

Then, all of a sudden, with no bloody warning (which is what all of a sudden means) when we are not wearing a protective wetsuit or flippers or a weight belt, they appear and head straight for us.

It can be scary, especially if the goal actually looks like it will come true. If we hesitate, or wait to analyse the situation we can miss the opportunity and get a first class ticket to regret.

Sometimes we are the ones that dive under the goal and sometimes we move fast and then get out of the way at the last minute, sabotaging the opportunity and sometimes, just sometimes, our goals move so fast that we have no time to think and we just go for it and get to rejoice in the moment.

We saw dolphins off Main Beach two weeks later. I had flippers, mask and a wet suit this time but the dolphins did not hang around. I had a great snorkel though. I will add wild dolphins to my snorkeling dance card. Maybe next time I see them or maybe the time after that, whenever it is, I deserve it and I'll be ready.

P.S. You are no longer supposed to try to swim towards whales. I'm not sure if the whales have been told this.

23

First Steps: If You Can't Walk Properl…

I sincerely hope that no parent ever says, "If you can't walk properly, don't walk at all" to their toddler. In my world, every clumsy awkward attempt to walk was praised and encouraged. There is no text book for what a baby's perfect first steps should look like except that they will be tentative and ungainly and preceded by bum plant after face plant after bum plant. They are always perfect.

'My child is walking now' is a big parental brag point. The month of the first unassisted stride is promptly rounded down and proudly proclaimed to anyone who will listen… okay, to anyone.

When a friend excitedly told me that his 10-month-old had taken his first steps on the day after his first birthday, I gave him a knowing smile and said, "Well… sucked in, Mate."

Sorry, that was what I thought. What I actually said was, "Congratulations." I may have snickered.

With Samuel, his first steps were very eagerly and somewhat naively anticipated. With our second child, Aelysha, there was not the same rush to get her walking. We knew that the momentary excitement of the solo half-stumble is balanced unevenly against the infant's suddenly extended range, insatiable increase in curiosity and their new found ability to run away from their parents. The ensuing baby proofing of a house also means that the contents of many cupboards and drawers will not be seen until the infernal clips are finally removed or destroyed.

Children have a number of pivotal movement milestones before they achieve independent perambulation. The baby going from the Tai Chi 'Stranded turtle on back' pose of immobility to being able to roll is a huge increase in mobility and this advancement is virtually guaranteed to be discovered by accident:

"Ok, I can do this, c'mon, c'mon... arms out front, brace arms. Use arms as a lever to lift my face off of the floor... good... hold on, dust bunny... gotcha. Yum. OK, but that is the last one, I don't want to spoil my appetite for boob juice.

OK... and on three... huh? Three? No idea what a three is. Aaaand, lifting. YES! Try to keep head steady... steady now... steady – ahhhhhh. WOW! What a great view from up here. That stuff over there looks like it needs rearranging. What? Another dust bunny? Left arm, left arm, no, no... leave it. Right arm you are supposed to know what... Augggh.

<SYSTEM ERROR: Balance system failure in progress. Left arm support absent. Head tilting. Falling sideways.>
Oh crap. Brace for the crash and WHAT? Right way up again? Resting on my tum. Oh, yeah.

Cheering? For me? What for? WOW! Hairy, smiley, smelly guy is very excited. Rolling? What is rolling? Oh… rolling. Yeah, totally nailed it. I'm a roller.

Wonder if I'll get this response every time I fall over? You want to see it again? Sure, I'll wait for you to get the camera."

The roller quickly becomes a crawler: slow and clumsy at first but then the infant gets spurred on by the obvious. They know that everything has its place and its place should be on the floor or in their mouth. Before long the crawl becomes a full nappy fuelled sprint. I am sure that they shouldn't be able to crawl so damn fast but they don't know that, so they do. Rapid crawling movement can also be accompanied by raucous laughter or extreme stealth, depending on the situation.

The final precursor to the solo right step, left step graduation is 'the Spiderman walk phase.' The baby walks on two legs but this is only achieved by holding onto a support; a parent's hand, a chair or a staircase. Pets are poor walking props as they have a strong tendency to rapidly move away from babies. Chubby little legs get stronger and stronger, until...

One day, in their own good time, the child needs to get from A to B but the quickest path is through open, barren ground. They will baulk and crawl across a few times or take the long way around the perimeter of the room UNTIL the moment when they finally string together a few milk-drunk steps that turns into an attempt at a short sprint. If you are very, very lucky, you will be their destination and you get to sweep them up in a huge hug and hold them tight and count yourself lucky for the simple blessing of being there for a gigantic milestone that is rapidly superseded.

A parent's hand for reassurance whilst walking is still welcome long after the child no longer really needs it. I remember with great fondness walking along a beach with Sam's little hand in mine as I, hunched down whilst burdened like a Sherpa with a backpack full of picnic paraphernalia and spare nappies as I tried to keep up with him. I was glad to be dragged along in the wake of his laughter and smiles and little spontaneous skips of joy.

With that trusting little hand in mine I know that I could have become 10 feet tall if I had needed to, to protect my boy. Thankfully I didn't need to and whilst the mama bear is rightly renowned for her ferocity in protecting its young, the papa bear can also be formidable. My heart goes out to places where even at 10 feet tall, some parents cannot protect their children.

Our walk on the beach added nothing to gross domestic product – it didn't get added to the 'baby steps whilst holding parents hand index' but it was one of so many little bonding moments that are priceless to me.

Before I knew it, that little hand outgrew my own. In the teenage years the young person's hand rarely, if ever, seeks out the comfort of the parent's hand. Understanding and knowing this, I refrain from seeking the reassurance, the physical connection that I would enjoy. There will be a time when that comes back. I am happy that I have so many priceless memories.

As a parent, my relationship with my children is constantly changing but my loving them never wavers even as I watch them fly the nest.

The training wheels are long gone and I can't run behind them holding onto the bicycle seat until they get their balance and accelerate away. Of course I knew this day was going to happen and I am happy and sad at the same time.

I remember teaching Sam how to drive a car. Obviously driving a car is different to taking first baby steps, isn't it? I mean, there is a right way to drive a car, isn't there? My way on the highway.

I loved having that unplugged time in the car with Sam when he was on his 'L' plates. He was a keen pupil because living in a regional part of NSW with virtually no public transport, driving was a ticket to a whole new level of freedom and mobility. Constantly asking parents to give you a lift to see friends gets real old real fast for everyone. The metaphor of me handing over the driver's seat to him was not lost on me.

We had a few challenges. I didn't ever say, "If you are not going to drive properly then don't drive at all." Not in those exact words. I mean he is a young adult now and driving a car is a lot different and much more dangerous than first steps. There are road rules, lots of rules some that I had forgotten and potential fines.

I shouldn't have said whatever I said. I don't remember the words but I know I was trying to be helpful. If only I had remembered a little about what I learned from when Sam first started to walk. A little praise can go a long way. Of course, the situation was very, very different. Carpet burn from a mis-step vs wrapping a vehicle around a light pole different.

Giddy praise for minutiae like turning on the ignition would have been madness and would not have helped make him a better or safer driver but what I forgot was that everything with driving was new to Sam. Being a passenger is not the same. Only pointing out what the trainee driver was doing wrong was not a good methodology. I wasn't even aware that I was doing that. My over active, concerned inner critic took over as my outer driving coach. Fortunately for me, Sam knew that I was very excited about him learning to drive and that my goal was to help him pass his test and be a safe driver.

Our mutual enjoyment of the learner driver process improved markedly when my student taught me to remember to acknowledge what is going right, as well as pointing out what can be done better. It is important for a new driver to know what they are doing well, so they can keep doing that. Obvious, but I had missed it.

Asking Sam how he felt he did executing that turn, that reverse park, that overtaking manoeuvre and listening to him before I made any comment also worked well. It was a great reminder for me to also acknowledge what I was doing well in my life, instead of constantly criticising myself (not for my driving, which is solid but for general stuff, ya know).

I am so grateful that Sam could talk to me about what bothered him when I was taking him driving instead of just sacking me as co-coach. Did I tear up a little when he drove away on his own for the first time? Yeah, a little, but his grin was as wide as the windscreen. He didn't drive into the horizon on that first drive, as nice as that sounds, it was just to the local shops and back. That was years ago. His spot in our nest is now empty and we miss him.

Sam is in the driver's seat for his life. He has plugged into his personal Sat-Nav. No doubt he will take a few turns that will take him to unexpected places. It is possible to get stuck on roundabouts and to get temporarily lost too. I know I did.

We have lit a perpetual, virtual candle in the window of the house we call home. It is our beacon to our child. Beth and I are the light keepers, always ready, to tend the dual purpose light that can both guide our young man home or just provide the reassurance, that no matter how far away he is, he is loved.

First steps to first drive to flying the nest. What a journey.
There are many pivotal moments in the continuum of movement that is a lifetime. Best shared.

Good to focus on what is going right.

24

Great Parental Expectations

Boys love trains: Girls I discovered, not so much. My ten year research project on this subject is based on an admittedly small sample size of one boy and one girl but I think that I am on the right track.

When Sam was little he loved trains, particularly steam trains. I like steam trains too but; 1) I never realised it before I became a dad and 2) I never loved them enough to pay $27.95 for a video but I loved Sam enough to invest in a number of VHS's that have now been deposited in a tip. I've had a lot worse investments.

Sam and I played with trains on the beach, on the water and in the air (yes, some trains can fly, d'uh). We were very Churchillian in our train games. We did not discriminate and played equally with wooden, plastic, metal and imaginary railways.

Despite all my misgivings, Thomas the Tank Engine and his capricious, back stabbing and 'naughty' friends were well represented in our toy box. As a tribute to Asterix and Obelix I always referred to the 'Fat Controller' as the 'Well-Padded Controller.'

Sam was not allowed to watch TV for 8 years and before you condemn or exalt us just know that we were helped in this by having no TV reception. We had a TV but every show looked like it was filmed in a snow storm.

Meanwhile, back at the station, I loved 'training' with Sam. The great thing about playing with young children is that I could bury little nuggets of sarcasm that would never be uncovered by Sam. At least I kidded myself that my humor was hidden gold.

I was travelling quite a bit for work and would regularly buy a guilt engine when I arrived home. The 'Guilt Engine,' as I explained to Sam, is Thomas' little known friend that runs best on a Catholic or Jewish track. Kids don't get sarcasm, right?

So you get the picture; trains excellent, dinosaurs also very solid but finding a fully operational dinosaur is a lot harder than finding a running steam engine.

As a parent I want my children to be happy and I know that children love surprises. Their reactions are spontaneous and bursting with a contagious joy. Planning surprises is a fun thing to do.

We were living in Melbourne. A scenic restored railway, Puffing Billy, operated on weekends about an hour and a half's drive from where we were living, so Beth and I conspired to give Sam his first ride on a 'live' steam train.

All of us were very excited except for Sam because he didn't know about it. Beth and I had already banked the parental kudos we would get. In fact we were already receiving compound interest on our kudos. What could go wrong? Right?

Puffing Billy is a 37 tonne, 6-2-6 steam engine that pulls narrow gauge open carriages 25 kilometers through beautiful Victorian bush.

Unfortunately, our drive from home to Puffing Billy, took longer than planned. Beth and I tried to maintain good cheer as we fervently hoped that our surprise had not left the station without us.

When we finally arrived, the train hadn't departed but there were no passengers on the platform and the steam whistle was tooting, 'too late,' 'too late'. We half parked, half abandoned the car and raced to buy our tickets.

Our cunning surprise was heading for derailment. We paid and rushed Sam toward the train. Billy was doing some very heavy breathing, I mean puffing. There was a final whistle - we had only seconds to get onboard AND amazingly, it seemed that we were going to make it.

Five steps from the train, Sam froze. In our mad rush Sam had somehow dodged surprise and instead got ambushed by shock. Parentally we had totally not considered that trains on TV or as cartoons, do not give a true sense of size. Real steam engines, especially to a small child, can seem freaking massive, huge metal breathing things that are almost alive. Puffing Billy was snorting Billy. He was also leaving the station Billy.

Sam would not move. No amount of frenzied cajoling worked. Picking Sam up and carrying him on was an option but didn't feel right. He refused to go near the train. Disappointment caught the train but we didn't.

I realized as the train pulled away just how much I had been looking forward to the ride. My parental kudos credit account recalibrated and so did I. It was tough. My love for my boy made it possible.

I picked up Sam, hugged him, kissed him and carried him back to the car. After Beth and I took a few deep breaths we decided with Sam that we would meet the train in our car and follow it as best we could.

We had a fun family day driving in the beautiful Dandenong Ranges. It was just not the day we had expected which is a surprisingly common parenting phenomenon. We caught up with Billy and we had a picnic with him too, no hard feelings.

Parental expectations can be tricky to manage. I will never forget what Steve Biddulph, an inspiring psychologist and parent educator said: That in his experience, parents have in their heads an ideal child and that children have in their heads an ideal parent and that there is nearly always a gap. Mind the gap.

I mind the gap and love my children because in the teenage years, the doors will be closing and we will be asked to stand clear, for a while at least.

25

Father's Day Note for My First Born

You knew I was ready
I did not
I am eternally grateful that you are so smart
You helped me grow up
I didn't want to
And I knew it was time

I got my head right and loved you
When you were only a bump in Beth's belly
I read the Narnia series to you out loud
And then started reading it silently
Because it was faster ☺ and you are telepathic

Your umbilical cord snapped at birth
So I held you as you took your first breaths
That was not an accident
There are no accidents

I saw your first smile, maybe it was gas
But it was magical
Newborn, you fell asleep on my bare chest
Skin to skin, heart to heart

Safe, warm and loved you blissfully slept

We connected
And I disappeared
I surrendered to your unconditional love
And have never been the same since

The moment, or was it a lifetime? Passed
On you slept, skin to skin, heart to heart
Connected, forever connected
Father to son
That was over 20 years ago
I will never forget it

Know that I love you always
To the furthest stars and back
Only think of me and my love is there
Transcending distance and time
And all the joy, fun and wonder
That you shared so generously, circles you too

I still want to keep you safe and warm
And you are setting out on your own
As you walk forward
Your path will find you, ready or not
Just as you found me
I believe in you. You are awesome

I am always here for you
To talk to, to be with you when possible
To share the joys and laughter of life
And the difficult times too
For they are also part of life's journey

My life is so much richer for having you in it
You made me a father.
The day you were born
Was my first father's day
Best present ever
Thank you. Love you.

Parenting Books that I Love

All books written by Robin Grille:
http://www.our-emotional-health.com/about.html

Parenting for a Peaceful World by Robin Grille
Paperback or eBook: 500 pages
ISBN-13: 978-0992360405
Heart to Heart Parenting by Robin Grille
Paperback or eBook: 320 pages
ISBN-13: 978-0733322983
"Rewards and Praise: The Poisoned Carrot" by Robin Grille is a superb article from Parenting for a Peaceful World:
Gentle Birth, Gentle Mothering by Dr Sarah Buckley
Paperback or eBook: 352 pages
ISBN-13: 978-1587613227
http://sarahbuckley.com/gentle-birth-gentle-mothering
The Continuum Concept by Jean Liedloff
Paperback or eBook: 192 pages
ISBN-13: 978-0201050714
Raising Boys by Steve Bidulph & his other books too
Paperback or eBook: 216 pages
ISBN-13: 978-1607746027
The Five Love Languages of Teenagers by Gary Chapman
Paperback or eBook: 288 pages
ISBN-13: 978-0802473134
Siblings Without Rivalry by Adele Faber and Elaine Mazlish
Paperback or eBook: 288 pages
ISBN-13: 978-0393342215
Teen Stages by Ken and Elizabeth Mellor
Paperback or eBook: 224 pages
ISBN-13: 9781402215292
Beyond Discipline - From Compliance to Community, by Alfie Kohn
Paperback or eBook: 191 pages
ISBN-13: 978-1416604723
He'll be OK – Growing Gorgeous Boys into Good Men by Celia Lashlie
Paperback or eBook: 222 pages
ISBN-13: 978-0732284503

www.ingramcontent.com/pod-product-compliance
Lightning Source LLC
Chambersburg PA
CBHW070852050426
42453CB00012B/2151